The Ultimate Guide to Soil

The Ultimate

Guide to Soil

*The Real Dirt on Cultivating Crops,
Compost, and a Healthier Home*

Anna Hess

SKYHORSE PUBLISHING

COPYRIGHT © 2016
BY ANNA HESS

Skyhorse Publishing books may be purchased in bulk at special discounts for sales promotion, corporate gifts, fund-raising, or educational purposes. Special editions can also be created to specifications. For details, contact the Special Sales Department, Skyhorse Publishing, 307 West 36th Street, 11th Floor, New York, NY 10018 or info@skyhorsepublishing.com.

Skyhorse® and Skyhorse Publishing® are registered trademarks of Skyhorse Publishing, Inc.®, a Delaware corporation.

Visit our website at www.skyhorsepublishing.com.

10 9 8 7 6 5

Library of Congress Cataloging-in-Publication Data

Names: Hess, Anna, 1978- author.
Title: The ultimate guide to soil : the real dirt on cultivating crops, compost, and a healthier home / Anna Hess.
Other titles: Real dirt on cultivating crops, compost, and a healthier home
Description: New York : Skyhorse Publishing, [2016]
Identifiers: LCCN 2016003518 | ISBN 9781634507707 (pbk. : alk. paper)
Subjects: LCSH: Soils.
Classification: LCC S591 .H477 2016 | DDC 631.4--dc23 LC record available at http://lccn.loc.gov/2016003518

Cover design by Jane Sheppard
Cover photographs by Anna Hess

Print ISBN: 978-1-63450-770-7

Printed in China

Contents

Introduction

A Love Affair with Soil

Soil is at the heart of a healthy garden.

When my husband wants to make my day, he doesn't buy roses; instead, he comes home with a truckload of horse manure. On summer nights, he checks to see how much dirt is embedded in the soles of my perennially bare feet before allowing me into bed. And he looks on slightly bemused when I rush out during February thaws to weed the berry patch just for the sake of plunging my hands into rich, dark garden soil.

Most gardeners know where I'm coming from since they share my deep-seated attraction to dirt. Part of that fascination lies in the purely mechanistic understanding that good soil makes healthy plants and eases the labors of weeding. But are any of us really immune to the seductive aroma of actinomycetes wafting out of a deep loam? When we read that scientists are running controlled trials to determine how well another soil microorganism (*Mycobacterium vaccae*) works as an antidepressant by tricking our brains into producing extra serotonin, are we really surprised?

Joel Salatin likes to say that he's a grass farmer, but for most of us, soil is the ultimate heart of our garden and homestead. Luckily, that heart is easy to nurture. A few easy changes to our usual gardening routines will create soil so resilient and healthy that bountiful, nutrient-dense harvests become a fact of life.

In my own garden, I've used the tips and tricks in this book to turn overfarmed, waterlogged, eroded ground into black gold that forms the focus of a vibrant homestead. And if you keep reading, your garden's journey back to good health will be even faster and simpler than mine was. So why wait? Nurture your soil and reap the rewards of nourishing, homegrown fruits and vegetables today!

The Big Picture

Each year, sorghum-sudangrass hybrids sequester three times as much carbon per acre as is packed away by a mature deciduous forest.

If feeding your garden's soil isn't a lofty enough goal for you, here's something to consider—agricultural soil is one of the easiest places to sequester carbon in an effort to fight climate change. Every time your soil turns one shade blacker, that's carbon dioxide you've pulled out of the air and put to work where it can't melt glaciers and raise sea levels.

So how do you maximize your garden's ability to pack on the carbon? Simply changing over to no-till practices sequesters 90 to 230 pounds of additional carbon per acre per year, but cover crops are the real heavy hitters. A planting of oilseed radishes will pump a massive 3,200 pounds of carbon per acre per year into the ground . . . while still leaving you all summer in which to grow tomatoes! That's equivalent to the amount of carbon sequestered in a 120-year-old northeastern woodland of the same size. But why stop there? Sorghum-sudangrass hybrids triple oilseed radish's humus-building powers, sequestering up to 10,565 pounds of carbon per acre into the earth and creating topsoil so rich that earthworms will go nuts.

The great thing about the carbon sequestration powers of soil is that every trick you use to sequester carbon does double-duty by improving your garden's health and allowing you to grow more food with less work in a smaller space. In the end, if you get to work improving your soil's organic-matter levels, then that organic matter will get to work for you . . . and for the world.

What to Do if Your Soil Isn't So Friendly

I can just hear some of you griping, "Yes, dark, fluffy garden soil sounds wonderful! But my dirt is so terrible that when I plant cover crops, the buckwheat only gets three inches high before giving up the ghost. How am I supposed to build soil if even cover crops refuse to grow?!"

Unfortunately, most of us aren't lucky enough to start out with high-quality soil. If you live in the city or are trying to

Six months after building high-raised beds and amending with rotted chicken bedding, a formerly waterlogged wasteland was growing luscious tomatoes.

garden close to a new house site, you may be facing compacted subsoil masquerading as topsoil. Or perhaps you bought an old farm like I did where the former owner's mismanagement caused all of the topsoil to completely erode away and where a high water table turns your garden into a swamp. You may be fighting clay that becomes hard as a rock during summer droughts. Or maybe your soil is so sandy that every time you water, the ground is parched again half an hour later.

Don't despair—all of those problems can be fixed. Just so you know where I'm coming from, let me explain that farmers judge soil based on land-capability classes, a rating system that begins at 1 (excellent) and runs all the way to 8 (terrible) based on potential agricultural uses of that land. Classes 1 and 2 are perfect for row crops, 3 can sometimes be used for row crops but is better for hay, classes 4 through 6 are generally considered only good for pasture, and farming is not recommended on classes 7 and 8. With that information in mind, you should know that my garden is divided into two different capability classes—my "good" soil is class 4, with the caveat that depth to the water table is often as little as one foot, while my poor soil is class 7 (not recommended for farming).

And yet, despite the deck being stacked against us, my husband and I have created vibrant, healthy garden ecosystems using both types of soil found on our land. In fact, we manage to feed ourselves all the vegetables we eat in a year using that same un-garden-worthy soil.

The reason I tell you this is to help overcome any pessimistic vision you might have of your own plot of earth. No matter what your starting point looks like, you *can* improve your growing space and harvest as much food as you wish as long as you put the health of the soil first.

So how do you take worn-out dirt and plant an edible paradise? The answer is simple—fix any structural problems (like compaction or a high water table), get the nutrients into balance, then build humus like mad. The rest of this book shows you how to do just that.

PERSONALITY TESTS FOR YOUR SOIL

Looking, smelling, and squeezing can give you critical insights into the health of your garden soil.

Most soil books feel obliged to begin with several long, grueling chapters about the chemistry and biology of soil. And while my geeky side finds those topics intriguing, I have to admit that my eyes glaze over as I work my way through formulas for bulk density and as I peruse long-winded descriptions of the nitrogen cycle.

On the other hand, my ears perk back up when I consider aspects of soil science that relate directly to my own garden. Perhaps you also want to know about the soil traits that you can feel, see, smell, and change. If so, then the following chapters are a great place to start since I'll focus on the tangible elements of your dirt that you can analyze using simple, at-home tests that will cost you nothing except a little bit of your time.

When you're done figuring out your soil's personality the easy way, you may decide to read more deeply about some of these topics. If so, *Soil Science & Management* by Edward J. Plaster should be your first stop since this textbook is easy to read and colorfully illustrated despite being geared toward use in college classes. *Teaming with Microbes* by Wayne Lewis and Jeff Lowenfels is also a must-read if you're specifically interested in the tiny soil critters that are too small to see with the naked eye but that impact everything from the availability of plant nutrients to the texture of your soil. I've also included information about several other relevant books in the Appendix.

But, for now, let's leave those mind-numbing details to the scientists and find out what a gardener really wants to know about her soil—whether it's ready to grow tasty tomatoes. So pull on your mud shoes and get ready to dirty your fingernails as you feel your way toward better soil health.

Chapter 1:
The Big Picture

Weeds and Growability

Nitrogen-fixing plants, like this black locust, are a sign of soil low in nutrients.

Photo credit: Adrianne Hess

As gardeners, our primary interest in soil quality usually stems from our yearning to grow beautiful flowers or delicious fruits and vegetables. So it makes perfect sense to begin our soil adventure by peering more closely at the plants already growing on our patch of earth. However, while you might be inclined to consider your rose bushes or cucumber vines, I instead recommend taking a look at the state of less spectacular species—the weeds hovering at the edges of the garden plot or growing in the aisles beneath your feet.

Why weeds? In contrast to your crop plants, these overlooked species are much less likely to be plagued by insects or diseases, so you won't get hung up on a dwindling specimen whose ills have nothing to do with the state of the earth. In addition, plant species often become weeds precisely because they're able to thrive in low-nutrient conditions that would make a squash vine curl up and die. So if even your weeds aren't thriving, you know you're really in trouble.

The difficulty with using weeds as an indicator of soil health is that the plants springing up in neglected gardens are very region-specific. Here in the mountains of southwest Virginia, I know that patches of tall blackberry canes are a good sign—yes, they'll be hard to eradicate when the time comes to plant my garden, but these brambles tend to grow where soil is rich and deep. On the other hand, if an area has been left alone for more than a decade and all it managed to grow was a few scraggly black locusts or a stand of browned broomsedge, I know there's something amiss.

Of course, black locusts are primarily found in the southern Appalachian mountains, so if you live elsewhere, you're going to have to figure out your own indicator plants. The generalities tend to hold true, though. Nitrogen-fixing plants (mostly legumes, but also a few other species like autumn olives, sea buckthorns, and alders) thrive in very poor soil where nothing else can find enough fertility to grow. Sedges and rushes enjoy wet, waterlogged ground, while mosses thrive in heavy shade. On the other hand, vibrant growth of most other types of plants probably means your soil is in pretty good shape.

But what about the smaller herbaceous weeds that inevitably pop up between your strawberry and asparagus plants? Some gardeners firmly believe that their most common garden weeds indicate a deficiency in the soil and that the weeds would naturally disappear if the proper nutrient was supplied. Or, as Ehrenfried Pfeiffer wrote in the 1970 classic *Weeds and What They Tell Us*: "Weeds are indicators of our failure."

Pfeiffer used a nuanced approach to place weeds in suites that indicate overarching problems giving those particular species a leg up. For example, if your garden is overrun with docks, horsetails, and hawkweed, Pfeiffer's system would indicate that your plot suffers from overly acidic soil. But simply finding one of those species in your garden is a less clear sign of a pH imbalance. The table on the next page summarizes three common soil problems and the associated weedy species that enjoy each condition, based on Pfeiffer's book.

If your garden is overrun with a certain type of weed, the plant might be pointing out a deficiency in the soil. However, the overabundance is more likely to stem from that classic homestead disease—gardener neglect.

Indicator plants for three common soil problems

Acidic soil (often linked to poor drainage)	Crusted soil or hardpan	Overcultivated soil with excessive nitrogen
sorrels, docks, fingerleaf weeds, lady's thumb, horsetail, hawkweed, and knapweed	field mustard, horse nettle, penny cress, morning glory, quackgrass, chamomile, and pineapple weed	lamb's quarter, plantain, chickweed, buttercup, dandelion, nettle, prostrate knotweed, prickly lettuce, field speedwell, rough pigweed, common horehound, celandine, mallow, carpetweed, and thistles

Unfortunately, while I love the idea of weed infestations being a cue toward deciphering soil problems, my own experience has shown that common garden weeds like the ones listed above are almost always linked to gardener neglect. In other words—the thistles we fought for the first several years we farmed were entirely due to me missing the boat and allowing a single plant to go to seed during year one. Trying to blame my infestation on excessive nitrogen wouldn't have been nearly as effective as heading out with a shovel to dig up next year's plants before they had time to bloom. (Yes, we did finally get rid of those thistles . . . and my bare feet really appreciated it.)

Whether you use specific suites of weeds to point out soil issues or whether you simply look at overall growability of the wild plants invading your garden edges, it's worth spending a minute walking through your garden and peering at the plants you didn't intend to grow. And if you notice a problem, hopefully one of the tests that follow will help nail down the specifics. Wouldn't it be great if you could tell your friends that your carrot harvest is ten times as bountiful this year . . . all because of the weeds?

Where Did Your Soil Come From?

Now that you've gotten a very general idea of the health of your garden soil, it's time to zoom in on the specifics that make your own patch of earth unique. This section isn't so much a hands-on test as a look at where your soil originated and how that origin influences the dirt you work with today. So if you're itching to get some grime beneath your fingernails, feel free to skip this section and move on to the next test.

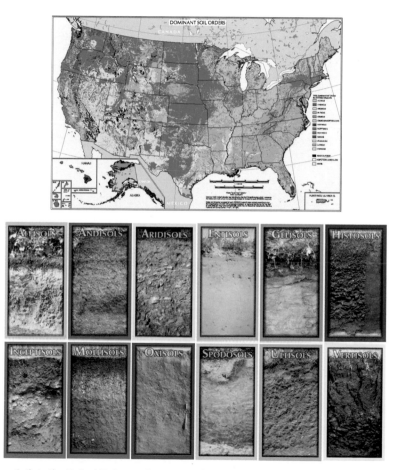

Soils in the United States can be organized into twelve orders. Map and photos courtesy of the US Department of Agriculture.

Soil orders in the United States

Soil order	Primary US location	Origin	Description	Good for agriculture?
Alfisol	Midwest	Moist, temperate deciduous forests	Organic matter near the surface above light-colored topsoil, then clayey subsoil	Yes
Andisol	Pacific Northwest, Hawaii, and Alaska	Volcanic glass	Dark in color and light in weight with lots of organic matter and with the ability to hold copious water	Yes, but binds phosphorus and leaves little available for plants
Aridisol	Southwestern states	Deserts	Often alkaline and salty	Somewhat. Must be irrigated, and then can have problems with salt buildup.
Entisol	Scattered, mostly in the Rocky Mountains	On top of very resistant rocks, or in climates that lessen weathering or promote erosion	Young soils that lack a distinction between the topsoil and subsoil	No

Soil orders in the United States (cont.)

Soil order	Primary US location	Origin	Description	Good for agriculture?
Gelisol	Alaska	Tundra, cold desert, or tall mountaintops	Permafrost in the subsoil, and often peat on the surface	No
Histosol	Northern Midwest and along the Atlantic and Gulf coasts	Anaerobic wetlands	Very high in organic matter (up to 30%). Commonly called peat or muck.	Yes, if drained. But large amounts of carbon dioxide are released during the drainage process.
Inceptisol	Scattered, mostly in the Pacific Northwest	Volcanic ash and other sources	Like entisols, but a bit more developed	No
Mollisol	Great Plains, some of Pacific Northwest, and parts of Iowa and Illinois	Grasslands	Deep, dark soils high in organic matter and minerals. The typically high microorganism populations create lots of soil aggregates, which increase fertility.	Yes

Soil orders in the United States (cont.)

Soil order	Primary US location	Origin	Description	Good for agriculture?
Oxisol	Puerto Rico and Hawaii	Tropics	Typically lacking organic matter and phosphorus. Containing lots of red or yellow, sand-like iron-oxide and aluminum-oxide clay particles in the subsoil.	No
Spodosol	Northeastern states and northern parts of the Midwest	Cool, moist coniferous forests	Acidic, light-colored soils that are stained dark in the subsoil by iron or aluminum. The soils tend to leach and to be low in nutrients.	No, except for blueberries. Can be managed with lime and fertilizers to grow other crops.
Ultisol	Southeast	Warm, humid areas	Similar to oxisols, but not quite as weathered. Subsoil is usually acidic and full of reddish clay.	Somewhat. Can be productive if properly limed and fertilized.
Vertisol	South-central states	Areas with cycles of wet and dry periods	Clay soil that shrinks when dry and swells when wet, creating large cracks and mixing the soil so layers don't form	Yes, although the soil can be hard to till

Still here? Okay, let's talk geology. Because that's where your soil originated—with the rocks that make up the earth's crust. Over hundreds or thousands of years, wind, ice, and rain slowly broke down each area's bedrock into tiny particles that became soil, and the type of daughter soil resulted directly from the type of parent rock. For example, if your land lies atop limestone, your soil is bound to be high in calcium (and sometimes magnesium), which leads to alkaline soil with a high pH. Sandstone, unsurprisingly, turns into sand, and shale turns into silt and clay.

However, the effects of your bedrock only go so far because soils formed in place are much less common than soils carried from elsewhere via the action of wind, water, glaciers, or gravity. The classic example is the Great Plains, which contain some of the United States' most fertile soil. This region is home to wind-born silt (also known as loess) that blew south as ancient glaciers receded and left bare soil behind where ice once lay. In New England, the results of glacial action are yet more obvious, but in this case gardeners see stones of varying sizes deposited in spots where glaciers melted, along with poorly drained ground in the sites of previous glacial lakes.

Water of the unfrozen variety is just as effective at forming and moving soil as glaciers are. Specifically, many parts of Minnesota, Wisconsin, Florida, Michigan, and Alaska are home to organic soils that formed underwater when plants and animals fell to the bottom of lakes and seas and only partially decomposed. Meanwhile, soils deposited by streams and rivers across the country tend to show up as sandy or gravelly earth at the bases of hills, which then give way to silty soil in floodplains. Finally, sandy soils are sometimes the result of quartz and sandstone broken down in place, but the sand might also have built up as part of marine sediments where ocean waves once crashed ashore.

If you're feeling geekily inclined, soil orders are one way of getting a big-picture idea of how the thousands of unique types of soil in the United Sates are classified. Mollisols, for example, include those wind-driven Great Plains soils, while spodosols in New England are poor soils that require lots of TLC if used as agricultural land, and ultisols are made up of that ubiquitous red clay in the southeast. Check out the map and table on pages 7–10 to see how your soil stacks up.

Broccoli Test

Checking the state of overwintering crop debris in early spring is a good way to assess the health of your soil's microbial community.

I'll end this big-picture chapter with a look at something very small but very important—microbes that you can't see with your naked eye. The idea behind this test is that healthy soil hosts lots of decomposing microorganisms that prevent even the most ornery debris from remaining unchanged in your garden for very long. And while I call the project a "broccoli test," you can use any type of overwintering crop debris in

By the beginning of April, broccoli stalks should be easy to pull out of the ground, and they should splinter between your fingertips without much effort.

order to assess your microbial populations. For example, corn and okra stalks cut back last fall or autumn broccoli, cabbage, and brussels sprout plants abandoned after the year's final harvest are all worth evaluating since these plants are woody enough to require some microbial muscle before they'll fade back into the soil.

Timing is as important in this test as selecting the proper plant to tug on. To make your assessment when it counts, head into your garden in early spring (about April first here, or whenever you plant your initial bed of uncovered lettuce), and take a look at the remains of last year's vegetable crops. What you want to see is bleached, brittle stems that release readily from the earth with one mild tug and can then be splintered apart between your thumb and forefinger with only a modicum of pressure. Corn stalks tend to latch into the soil a bit harder than broccoli roots do, but at least 90% of even the previous year's final corn planting should be easy to pull loose from the ground by the first of April.

What makes this magic happen? The decomposers in your soil range from microscopic bacteria and fungi all the way up to sowbugs and worms. And even though it's fun to know exactly who does what and how to identify each species in a handful of earth, the important point is determining whether you have enough healthy critters to get the job done.

So if your corn stalks are still firmly rooted and last year's mulch didn't rot at all over the previous winter, it's time to get serious about soil health. Most of the techniques in this book will help improve your microbial life, but I specifically recommend transitioning over to a no-till system, making sure there's sufficient nitrogen in your ground, and maintaining proper moisture levels in an effort to keep your decomposers happy.

But don't skip ahead just yet. There's still a lot to learn about your garden's unique soil profile. So turn the page and prepare to get even dirtier as we delve into soil texture.

Chapter 2:
Soil Aggregates

Carrot Test

Carrot shapes are influenced by soil texture.

Moving on from the biological to the physical, we'll also change seasons to summer and crops to carrots. You might have already noticed the differences in shape between carrots grown in different parts of your garden. For example, did you ever dig up a bed of carrots and find that all of the roots had split and twisted into a jumbled mess? Sometimes, carrots curl around each other because you didn't thin the crop sufficiently. But splitting, gnarled carrots that aren't closely intertwined are generally a sign that your soil is either compacted or is full of pebbles and rocks.

Compacted soil (on the right) lacks both the small and the large pores that allow roots, rain, and air to move efficiently through the earth. Often, a hardpan layer (darker brown in the drawing, but not distinguished by color in actual soil) develops just beneath the level that a plow or rototiller can reach.

What do I mean by compacted soil? Even though the earth seems solid when we're striding across it, as soon as you start peering closely at the dirt, you'll notice lots of air spaces between the grains. Unfortunately, it's relatively easy to mash your soil down so those air spaces disappear, a process known as compaction.

Simply walking on your garden soil can remove air spaces, which is why many gardeners create permanent aisles and beds, concentrating all of their foot traffic in certain sacrifice zones. Traditional tilling also creates compaction issues, especially if your soil is heavy or if you till when the ground is too wet or too dry. So your first step in dealing with compaction is changing your own habits so the problem won't come back.

What's next? You can physically fluff up soil with the broadfork, a tool that opens up spaces between soil particles without turning the layers of the earth. But before you rush out and buy expensive tools, I should tell you that moderately compacted soil often responds just as well to the action of biotillage cover crops like oilseed radishes. These deep-rooted plants easily push their roots through hard layers of soil, leaving biopores behind after they rot in place and increasing soil organic-matter levels in the process.

Okay, I know I just threw a technical term at you, but biopores are pretty easy to understand (and even to see in your soil). These large air channels start at the surface of the ground and run several feet into the earth, turning the openings into superhighways for soil-dwelling critters like earthworms. Meanwhile, biopores give roots quick access to other parts of the earth profile and also make it easier for rain to infiltrate deeply rather than running off during deluges. Finally, biopores promote faster carbon dioxide and oxygen exchange between the air in your soil and the air above, which helps encourage the aerobic microorganisms who do such good work decomposing organic matter and providing nutrients for your crops.

Photo credit: Briar Cooper

The easiest way for a gardener to see soil-pore formation in action is to take away one of the boards supporting the side of a raised bed. You'll likely notice earthworm channels, smaller pores that follow roots, and the crumbly structure of good soil.

Biopores aren't the be-all and end-all of soil structure, though. In fact, much smaller channels between soil aggregates are just as important for healthy crops. These minuscule pathways do some of the same work as biopores, helping with air exchange and water management for example. But the smaller air cavities work a bit differently—rather than helping rain soak into the earth, mini-pores ensure that your soil can hold onto the falling water so all of the moisture doesn't drain away between storms. Small channels also allow water to move upwards from the groundwater into the root zone during droughts via capillary action, so they're doubly important for ensuring your crops find enough water to grow and thrive.

What can a gardener do to produce these essential, tiny channels between soil aggregates? The best solution is to add lots of organic matter and then beg your soil microorganisms to do the work for you. In fact, spreading mulches and other amendments directly onto the soil surface is like putting up a sign reading "Seeking earthworms—apply within." Worms will inevitably show up eat the tasty treats in situ, then they'll poop out high-nutrient castings deeper in the earth. And while moving between the two locations, the worms create— you guessed it—holes in the soil for roots and air to follow.

A third type of even smaller pore is created when minuscule soil particles are chemically bound together into aggregates, which range in size from nearly too small to see all the way up to several inches in diameter. These aggregates usually begin forming when roots or fungi increase in girth while thrusting their way through the soil, an act that pushes soil particles together on either side of the roots or fungal hairs. This slight compression of the soil is then cemented into more long-lived aggregates when microorganisms eat nearby organic matter and create gummy secretions to bind the soil particles in place. Next, calcium ions in the soil bind small aggregates together into larger particles known as peds.

Okay, that got a bit technical, but the bottom line is simple. Tiny air channels in soil form between soil aggregates, and soil aggregates form due to living things like roots and fungi doing their job deep in the earth. Larger pores form along earthworm channels, and yet more massive channels are due to the work of deep-rooted crops.

In the end, promoting healthy critters promotes healthy soil. And healthy soil means straight, unbranched carrots—gotta love it when you can eat your report card!

Muddy-Water Test

A: new soil

C: established soil

B: established soil

Note lumps of unincorporated clay in soil A.

Aggregates in more established soil are subtly different.

Moistening a sample of your garden soil makes it easier to see the aggregates.

The carrot test gives you a rough idea of the texture of your soil, but you can explore several aspects of this characteristic more directly with just a little expenditure of elbow grease. We'll start with an easy way to assess soil aggregates—the muddy-water test.

To begin, fill a glass with water and then gently drop in a few spoonfuls of soil straight from your garden. Stir the soil-water mixture for a few seconds, then drain off any excess water. Finally, decant the mud that remains in the bottom of your glass onto an absorbent surface, like a piece of wood.

If you smooth the wet dirt gently with your fingers, you should see one of two things. The first possibility is that your soil will look like sand at the beach, with all of the particles small and roughly the same size. This is bad news since it means your soil texture depends solely on the original mineral particles present, with no aggregation due to the action of worms and microbes. In this case, the quick fix is to add lots of organic matter in the form of compost, then to grow cover crops in an effort to tempt your soil biology into binding those particles together.

If your soil isn't pure sand and if you've been gardening in that spot for a while, you're more likely to notice several different particle sizes represented on your piece of wood. Now look closely at the biggest lumps. Does each large mass appear to consist of lots of smaller lumps of varying sizes and colors glued together, or are the lumps simply clods of clay like you might see in a garden that was tilled when wet?

You can get an idea for the differences between these two scenarios by studying the images on page 19. My soil sample A consists of poor soil that began as subsoil mounded up into a quick raised bed two years prior to being photographed, while the other two samples came from more established garden plots with superior aggregation. In sample A, lumps of unincorporated clay are visible despite the fact that I've added a moderate amount of organic matter and have grown some cover crops in that patch in the years since I created the beds. In fact, now that I've peered more closely at soil A using a muddy-water test, I'm unsurprised that these garden beds don't yet produce the way I'd like them to.

Soil aggregates are visible to gardeners as a healthy crumb structure that looks a bit like fluffy, homemade bread.

In contrast, soil sample C was a good, loamy soil even when I began gardening nine years ago and the mixture of soil-particle sizes attests to that fact. The more interesting sample to consider is soil sample B, which I include in an effort to hearten anyone who's starting a garden from scratch on poor ground. Soil B was identical to soil A when we first moved to our farm, but copious additions of manure and mulch, no-till practices, and several rounds of cover crops have transitioned poor soil into a vibrant, healthy growing space in the interim. And the muddy-water test reflects that transformation. If anything, soil B looks the best of the three samples I photographed from both a color and aggregate perspective, proving that a bit of TLC is all it takes to turn bad soil into good.

Crusting and Clods

A soil crust on the left and clod on the right are both caused by a combination of disturbance and water.

For this next test you'll need to get down on your hands and knees and peer at the dirt in situ, hunting for two potential problems that are both man made. Clods are usually immediately visible since they consist of dried-together clumps of earth that stick up above the soil surface, but a crust might not be discernible until you poke at the skin of the earth with your fingertip. Is the surface loose and crumbly, or is there a more solid layer that ranges from a tenth of an inch to two inches thick? If you notice the latter scenario, then your garden is the unhappy recipient of a soil crust. And like clods, crusts represent moderately bad news.

Both clods and crusts are more likely to form if your soil is high in silt or clay, but I'll leave the texture issue aside until the next chapter. In the meantime, you should understand that working your garden while the soil is excessively wet or dry can break apart those soil aggregates that I wrote so much about in the last section. And when soil aggregates break apart, it only takes a little bit of compaction to force them back together in a more rock-like fashion with no handy air holes in between to keep the soil loose. The result is clods, which make seedlings unhappy but tend to break apart naturally as rain and freezing temperatures level out the earth.

But why wait on nature to fix your soil problems when prevention is so easy? If you don't want clods, then don't till when the soil is more than lightly moist and don't harvest root vegetables or dig holes for perennial plantings at that time either. Meanwhile, even if you think the soil moisture is just right, you should always rake beds flat immediately after impacting the ground so bigger clumps won't dry together into impenetrable clods. Waiting until tomorrow for this final soil-conditioning step makes clods much more likely to develop.

Rapidly watering bare ground with a hose can cause soil crusts to form. To prevent this problem, break apart the liquid into smaller droplets using sprinklers or drip irrigation, and keep the soil surface covered with mulch.

In contrast to clod management, crust prevention takes a slightly keener eye. First of all, you need to understand how crusts form. These tough layers of surface soil often begin in gardens low in organic matter and with poor aggregate formation. Next, the gardener throws a monkey wrench at the earth by tilling the soil when the ground is too dry or by simply tilling too much. Either of these actions will break apart the few aggregates that are present, which in turn produces lots of tiny soil particles that quickly wash into pores in the soil surface during the next heavy rain. The result is a tough layer of surface soil that lets neither air nor water through, blocking those critical life forces from reaching the looser soil below.

Unfortunately, the presence of a soil crust creates a feedback loop that makes conditions grow worse and worse over time. First of all, since the blocked pores prevent rain or irrigation water from soaking in, excess liquid tends to run off the soil surface and erode away the topsoil. Meanwhile, plants that could have helped break apart the crust have a hard time pushing their tender sprouts through the hard surface layer, so seedlings often perish before they really begin to grow. The result is less organic matter in the soil, which leads to more crusting and erosion, to lack of aggregation, and to even lower organic-matter levels—bad news.

If you pay attention, though, crusts are extremely easy to fix. On the garden scale, you can simply drag a metal rake across the soil surface then mulch heavily and your problem will be solved. Next, change over to no-till practices and you'll probably never see a crust again.

My own experiences prove how an about-face in soil management quickly make crusts a thing of the past. As you'll soon see, my soil is very heavy and used to be prone to crusting when we used a rototiller to prepare new garden beds. But since tweaking my gardening practices, crusts became so rare that I had to scour my entire garden to come up with the photo that led off this section. I finally tracked down a flowerbed I'd recently built out of subsoil directly under runoff from my porch roof. But the remainder of my growing space—even including areas that are currently mulch-free because new seedlings are working their way out of the ground—hasn't seen a crust in nearly a decade.

Erosion

In the eastern United States, water is the leading cause of erosion.

I'll end this chapter with a soil problem I really hope you never see in your garden—erosion. The early stages of erosion can be relatively subtle, with topsoil washing or blowing away during heavy storms. But as the problem progresses, even the most neglectful farmer will notice that gullies are being dug into his earth.

The best solution to erosion is prevention. Always keep your soil covered, preferably with living plants that include cover crops during the off season. Or if winter oats and rye simply don't fit into your garden year, a heavy mulch is the next best choice for fallow-season erosion control. Meanwhile, boosting organic-matter levels will help as well since humus allows rain to soak into the ground even during downpours rather than puddling on the surface and then washing your topsoil away.

In contrast, tilling will exacerbate the effects of both wind- and water-based erosion since churning up the soil breaks apart aggregates that keep your topsoil anchored to the ground. Some of you may not be able to go no-till, though, in which case you can at least choose to plow in the spring rather than preparing the soil in the autumn and leaving the loose earth uncovered during winter rains. Similarly, sloped gardens will erode much more readily than flat land, so I recommend tilling along the contour so water will pool in the furrows rather than creating gullies running downhill from the highest point.

Massive dust storms in the 1930s were the result of deep plowing, drought, and high winds.

I've been writing about water up to this point because those of us in the eastern United States track most of our erosion back to heavy rains. Those of you in the drier West, though, will find that wind takes over where water leaves off. In fact, if you've seen images of the huge dust storms that spread across the prairie states during the Great Depression, you've seen the worst of wind erosion at work. That's definitely a human-created disaster we don't want to repeat.

Luckily, preventing wind erosion isn't rocket science. As with water erosion, cover crops and mulches do a great job of counteracting the scouring power of wind. Similarly, if you need to till, you should do so perpendicular to the prevailing wind just like you'd till on contour to lessen the erosive power of water. Finally, planted windbreaks can shield areas up to ten times as wide as the windbreak is tall, making them an excellent long-term approach to preventing your own local dust bowl.

The fact that you're reading this book means that you're probably too on-the-ball to allow erosion to grip your garden, whether wind or water is your local curse. But you may still be dealing with the results of previous owners' neglect if certain parts of your property seem to go straight to clay subsoil with little or no dark topsoil to be found. Don't worry—you're not alone. My farm was eroded down to subsoil before I bought the place, and as a result I've developed lots of ways to turn back the clock to a happier era. Later chapters will offer solutions that range from boosting organic matter with cover crops to lifting your growing zone out of the groundwater with high raised beds. So don't despair. Even if man-made problems not of your doing plague your garden plot, you're ingenious enough to fix them all!

Chapter 3: Soil Type

Ribbon Test

To begin the ribbon test, moisten a sample of soil and roll it into a ball.

By this point in your soil explorations, you're probably starting to notice that your soil's texture involves a lot more than simply the way the pieces of dirt are bound together into aggregates. This test and the one that follows will help you assess the underlying texture of your soil based on the percentages of three particle types—sand, silt, and clay. I'll write in more depth about these particles in a minute, but let's start by looking and feeling before we embark on book learning. So, once again, it's time to head out to your garden for some dirt and prepare to get muddy with the ribbon test.

The first step in this soil-texture examination consists of adding drops of water to your soil sample until the earth resembles the consistency of a child's play putty. If you add too much water, don't worry—you can just mix in some extra dirt. On the other hand, if the soil is too dry, you should keep adding more water.

Putty-like yet? Okay, now it's time to knead your wet dirt around a bit to break apart any soil aggregates that want to stay together while also incorporating moisture more throughly into the soil sample. Then roll the damp earth into a ball that's roughly half an inch in diameter.

You may already be noticing your soil's texture at this early stage in the game. Does the ball feel slimy and coat your fingers with muddy goo? That's the smallest soil particle, clay, doing what it does best—filling in all the gaps. At the other extreme, sand (the largest soil particle) will make the outside of your ball of earth feel slightly or very gritty, with the level of grit related to the proportion of sand in your sample. Silt is the middle-sized particle, and you probably won't be able to identify it at this stage in the game.

But what if your fingers get muddy *and* the ball of soil is gritty? Chances are good that there will be at least some of each particle size—silt, clay, and sand—in your sample. So this first assessment is really a way of getting a handle on the relative amounts of each particle in your piece of earth rather than being a way to separate out silt, sand, and clay.

Use a light squeeze to test for sand.

Now that you've guessed at your soil's texture merely based on its feel between your fingertips, it's time to give your ball of earth a light squeeze between your thumb and forefinger. Very sandy soil will break apart at this point—in fact, pure sand might not have formed into a ball in the first place. A crack in an otherwise cohesive ball, as shown on the previous page, usually results from a lower level of sand in your soil. And, at the other extreme, a ball of pure clay won't change shape much at all beneath the squeeze test.

Press the ball into a thin ribbon until it breaks.

Next, roll the ball into a slightly oblong shape, then press the tip of the oblong into a flat ribbon. As you slowly work the ribbon up between your thumb and forefinger, the thin piece of soil will originally stand erect. But sooner or later, the ribbon will crack under its own weight and will fall to one side.

Measure the length of the ribbon to assess soil-texture type.

Ribbon-test results

Length of ribbon	Soil type
0	sand or loamy sand
Less than 1 inch	loam, silt, silt loam, sandy loam
1 to 2 inches	sandy clay loam, silty clay loam, clay loam
2 to 3 inches	sandy clay, silty clay, clay

To complete the ribbon test, measure the length of the soil that extruded between your thumb and finger before the crack, then use the table above to determine your soil type. Pure loams (which contain a relatively even proportion of sand, silt, and clay) along with soils dominated by silt will form very short or no ribbons, while clayey soils form longer ribbons. The soil pictured in the examples is a silt loam.

Jar Test

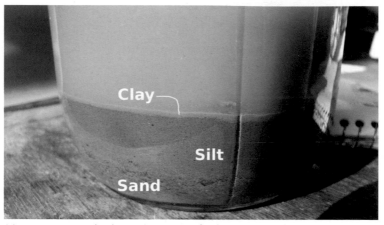

A jar test separates the three components of soil so you can make a visual assessment of their proportions.

If you don't want to get your hands dirty with a ribbon test, you can decipher the same information from a jar test. In this case, you begin by pouring about a cup of garden soil and two cups of water into a quart jar. Put on the lid and shake vigorously until the soil aggregates break apart, then let the container of muddy water sit for a day (or longer) until the various particles settle out.

After twenty-four hours, you should be able to see layers through the sides of the glass jar, as is shown in the photo above. Sand particles are the largest and heaviest particle, so they drop to the bottom fastest, followed by silt and finally clay. In fact, the smallest clay particles may remain suspended in the water for quite a long time, but it's okay to finish your test twenty-four hours after taking the sample.

Once you're ready to take measurements, use a ruler to figure out the exact height of each layer within your jar. For example, your sand layer might be a quarter of an inch deep, your silt layer one inch deep, and your clay layer a tenth of an inch deep. Using those measurements, the next step is to calculate the percent sand, silt, and clay within the total soil sample using the formula below.

Soil particle percentage = $\dfrac{\text{Inches of the soil particle}}{\text{Inches of sand + Inches of silt + Inches of clay}}$ X 100%

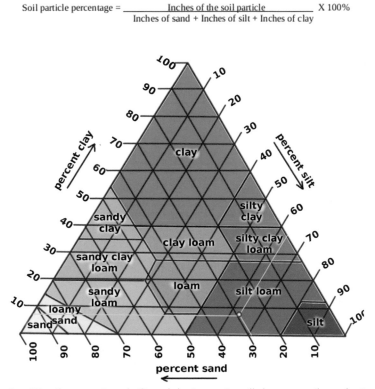

Inputting the percent sand, silt, and clay in your jar will place your soil sample at a specific spot on this triangle.

With those three numbers on hand, a soil triangle like the one shown above will pinpoint your soil texture. Just start on any side and work your way into the middle. For example, my jar test showed that the soil I was testing contained 29% sand, 64% silt, and 7% clay. So I located 29% sand on the bottom of the triangle and 7% clay on the left side of the triangle. Drawing straight lines parallel to the marks on those sides, my soil sample also matched up with 64% silt automatically. The dot where all three lines intersect shows my soil type— silt loam, just like the ribbon test suggested.

So what do you do with these assessments of soil texture? First, hope your soil turns out to be loam! As I mentioned earlier, loams contain a relatively even helping of all three types of soil particles, which makes them the sweet spot for easy gardening. Anything outside the loam category is more of an extreme soil that will require extra TLC to promote optimal productivity.

That said, sandy soils initially feel like you've hit easy street. The large particles result in large pores, which make the earth well-aerated, well-drained, and easy to work. Sandy soils also tend to promote early growth of spring crops like lettuce and carrots, and they're great for root crops in general since potatoes and turnips (for example) don't have such a hard time pushing through tough earth to make space for their massive below-ground portions.

On the other hand, water tends to flush through sandy soil too quickly for plants to stay properly hydrated unless you add large quantities of organic matter, meaning that sandy soils dry out quickly between rains. Meanwhile, the extra air within all of those large pores allows decomposing microbes to work like gangbusters, so organic matter decomposes too quickly in sandy soil and produces little stable humus. As a result, sandy soils are very good candidates for no-till operation, and they tend to respond well to the application of heavy mulches and biochar as well. You might also try out the sunken pit gardens I write about in chapter 7 if you suffer from sandy soil and a droughty climate.

At the other extreme, clay gets a bad rap because this type of soil tends to be poorly drained and difficult to work, then forms rock-hard lumps if tilled wet and allowed to dry. All of these characteristics are due to the very small pores that form between equally small clay particles. On the other hand, clay has its own unique benefits since the tiny particles bond nutrients to their surfaces much more readily than either sand or silt, meaning that both organic and natural fertilizers

This photo shows two classic solutions to heavy clay soil—raised beds and cover crops.

are more effective in clay soil than in sand. In general, clay tends to make gardens productive . . . if you can handle the heaviness and damp.

As with very sandy soil, my prescription for dense clay is adding lots of compost to the garden. Extra organic matter will help the tiny clay particles bond into larger aggregates, which in turn creates bigger pores and allows better movement of both air and water. Meanwhile, raised beds are a good fit with clay soil since mounded up earth will dry out more quickly in the spring and will also warm up more rapidly, counteracting two of the disadvantages of gardens in heavy clay. Finally, all of the tips in the compaction section are handy for use with clay soil since this type of earth is most likely to need mitigation in that regard.

You don't hear gardeners talk about silt much, even though this soil type is more common than you might think. I suspect that most silt gardeners (like I once did) simply assume we're saddled with clay because the soil types appear similar on the non-microscopic level. On the other hand, silty soil can also be compared to loams since both provide a happy medium between wet, dense clay and high-and-dry sand, and it's true that medium-textured soils in general tend to produce the highest yields. However, unlike loams, silts erode easily due to the absence of clay's stickiness, making it especially important to keep silty soil covered at all times with crops or mulch.

Before I end this long-winded discussion of soil texture, I should address one common question gardeners often have—is it worth creating an artificial loam by adding large quantities of clay to sandy soil or sand to clayey soil? The answer is usually no, simply because the amount of earth you'd have to move is gargantuan. Assuming your plant roots extend 6.7 inches into the soil (a typical plow depth), then you'd need to add about 1.2 *million* pounds of sand to an acre of soil to turn pure clay into loam. That's nearly 3,000 pounds of sand per hundred square feet of garden soil—probably enough to break your back. Now you can see why I recommend adding organic matter instead for similar results with much less expenditure of energy. In the end, it just makes sense to improve soil texture with cover crops, compost, and mulch rather than with truckloads of sand.

Online Soil Surveys

Although it's not a hands-on test, I wanted to end this chapter with an introduction to soil surveys since tracking down this information is a surefire way to find out more about the texture and potential of your particular patch of earth. A decade ago, gardeners were forced to pick up a copy of their county's soil survey on paper at the local extension office, then they had to peruse huge paper maps and page through the attached booklets in search of information about their soil types. Luckily, the Internet age has made things much simpler.

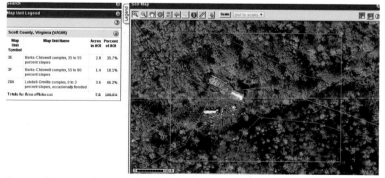

The Web Soil Survey is an online service of the Natural Resources Conservation Service that makes it easy for the average gardener to discover the types of soil found on her land.

Nowadays, all you have to do to find out your soil type is to go to the NRCS Web Soil Survey at http://websoilsurvey. sc.egov.usda.gov/App/WebSoilSurvey.aspx, zoom in to find and mark your area of interest, then click on the Soil Map tab to find out about each type of soil that's located on your property. More intensive, up-to-date instructions on using the NRCS Web Soil Survey tool can be found at http://websoilsurvey.sc.egov.usda.gov/App/HomePage.htm.

Our core homestead consists of three soil types, two of which differ only in their degree of slope.

Once you've figured out how to pull up your soil types (and I'll admit the process can be a little tricky), you'll end up with a map like the one shown on the previous page. Blue lines (incorrectly located on my soil map) indicate bodies of water while orange lines separate soil types. The map is also labeled with orange letters and numbers to signify different types of earth. These labels will vary from state to state, but in many areas the letter at the end of the soil type refers to the degree of slope. For example, soil type 3F is the same as 3E, but the former is located on a steeper part of the hillside.

If you click on the link for each soil type, the website will report the soil's properties in far more detail then you probably have any interest in reading. Some important factors to consider include:

Parent material: This is the basis of your soil and will be responsible for many of your soil's properties. For example, on my property, one soil type's parent material is "fine-loamy alluvium derived from limestone, sandstone, and shale," which means that the soil was carried by water off the surrounding hillsides (alluvium), and is thus likely to be quality topsoil. In addition, the fact that some of my soil began its life as limestone means that the plot tends toward alkalinity rather than acidity (although the sandstone and shale parent materials will mitigate that effect).

Typical profile: Imagine that you dug a hole from the soil surface down as far as you could go—the profile is the type of earth you'd find at each stage of your excavation. Most importantly, you can think of the first notation as the depth and type of your topsoil. For example: "0 to 6 inches: channery silt loam" means that the top six inches of my garden contain a relatively even proportion of silt, sand, and clay, but that its composition leans more toward silt.

Depth to restrictive feature: This usually tells you when or if the people who took the soil surveys hit bedrock during their sampling. If your garden shows bedrock less than 30 inches below the soil surface, then your soil is considered thin and you may have trouble growing trees and other deep-rooted plants. My shallower soil lists "20 to 40 inches to paralithic bedrock," while my deeper soil says "more than 80 inches." In both cases, I haven't had trouble with hitting bedrock.

Depth to water table: This is similar to the bedrock issue, but here the scientists were looking for standing water in the hole they dug. Once again, you'd like to have at least 30 inches in this category, although higher water tables can be managed (as I'll explain in chapter 7).

Land-capability classification: As I mentioned in this book's introduction, land-capability classification is a broad way of looking at the suitability of your garden for agriculture. In addition to the numerical explanations I listed previously, I should also mention that your number may have a letter after it, such as E (prone to erosion), w (poorly drained or sometimes flooded), s (shallow soil or another factor making the ground hard to till), or c (influenced by climatic extremes, such as are found in deserts or tundra).

You may have to flip over to the "Soil Data Explorer" tab and within that to the tab for "Soil Properties and Qualities" if you want to delve deeper into the makeup of your soil. There you can find out what your dirt looked like before humans began farming the area, including the original pH and percent of clay, silt, and sand. This type of information is handy to consider in conjunction with a professional soil test or with any of the hands-on home tests in this book as a way of gaining a deeper understanding of your garden earth.

One final note: if your soil consists of a complex, the name will be hyphenated, like "Lobdell-Orrville complex." When soil scientists make maps, they can't distinguish areas smaller than about an acre and a half. As a result, more complex arrangements of soil are lumped together and the individual tract of land on your property might include one or the other of the two soil types, or possibly a combination of both. As a result, both types of soil will have their characteristics listed separately within the NRCS description. In the example above, Lobdell is a slightly deeper and better-drained soil than Orville, but is otherwise quite similar.

I should conclude this section by saying that if you don't like maps, you shouldn't worry about this information too much. As you can see, my hands-on tests provide much of the same information, so tracking down your soil type is more of an academic exercise than a necessity in the home garden. If it sounds like fun, feel free to delve deep into the website, but be aware that you can still grow great zucchini without ever learning the specific words for your garden's soil type.

Chapter 4:
Organic Matter
and Drainage

Worm Test

One easy way to discover how many worms are in your garden is to turn your hens into the plot and watch them go nuts over the found food.

I've mentioned organic matter several times in previous chapters, so now it's time for this important feature to get a chapter of its very own. And what better way to measure organic matter than by looking at worms, those creepy-crawlies that breed like crazy in rich earth?

Given that correlation, it's no wonder that many books recommend measuring the health of your soil with a worm test. They elaborate as follows: Simply dig a square of earth one foot per side and six inches deep, pick through to count your earthworms, and then assess the number of wrigglers. Ten or more worms means your garden passes the test; fewer worms means you've failed.

The trouble with this simplistic worm test is that there are many different types of earthworms, and each species' numbers also vary widely depending on the time of year in which you dug your hole. For example, in the cold of midwinter or during summer droughts, you might not find any worms at all even in prime garden soil. In contrast, a damp spring rain may bring dozens to the surface.

As a result, I use a much less official worm test—I just keep an eye out for wrigglers as I go about my usual garden duties. In the process, I've noticed that established garden plots with a healthy helping of organic matter mixed throughout the root zone tend to be home to medium-sized worms that live in the mineral soil itself. Newer garden areas where I'm boosting organic-matter levels by depositing lots of compost and mulch on the soil surface instead host much larger worms that can be seen slithering away when you disturb their work of carrying that top-dressed organic matter deep underground.

What I'm leading you toward is the fact that worm tests not only assess overall organic-matter levels, they also pinpoint the type of organic matter in your soil. Specifically, healthy soil should be full of humus, a term used to refer to stable organic matter that has decomposed until it became a mass of waxes and lignins bound together with microbial gums and starches. More worms likely means more humus, but you can also analyze the situation more directly both by looking for the diagnostic dark hue of humus and by sniffing for the rich odor of good earth.

What's the big deal about humus? As I've mentioned previously, organic matter mellows out all kinds of soils, helping sandy earth bank water during droughts, fluffing up clays so they're easier to manage, and buffering pH in both acidic and alkaline ground. Humus feeds microorganisms that create soil aggregates, holds onto nutrients so they don't leach out of the soil during heavy rains, and even helps the ground warm up more quickly in the spring due to the darker color.

Organic matter has other purposes as well. If you live in the city (or on the site of an old orchard or other type of heavily sprayed farmland), you'll want to boost organic matter as a preventative measure since humus tends to latch onto heavy metals and to hold those troublesome elements in place so they're less likely to enter your food supply. Meanwhile, in all types of soil, decomposing organic matter increases carbon-dioxide levels close to the earth's surface, which in turn stimulates plant growth. Finally, humus literally feeds your soil and plants with the most important nutrient of all—nitrogen.

Since organic matter is so integral to the garden, I'll write more about this soil characteristic in later chapters. But, for now, you can simply keep an eye out for worms in order to tell whether you've been feeding your garden enough compost and mulch. Then, if in doubt . . . pile on a little more.

Soil Color

As I mentioned above, good soil is dark brown or black due to the large amounts of organic matter present. But did you know that the soil particles making up most of the dirt beneath your feet are naturally white or completely lacking in color? Other hues usually appear when organic matter stains these particles brown or when various compounds add more brilliant colors to the soil.

Mineral effects on soil color

Color	Mineral source	Rich in:
Black	Iron sulfide	Iron and sulfur
Black	Todorokite	Manganese
Black, metallic	Pyrite	Iron and sulfur
Gray, dark	Glauconite	Varies
Gray, light	Quartz	Silicon
Brown, very pale	Gypsum	Calcium and sulfur
Red, dark	Ferrihydrite	Iron
Red	Hematite	Iron
Reddish-yellow or red	Lepidocrite	Iron
Yellow or brown	Geothite	Iron
Yellow, pale	Jarosite	Iron, potassium, and sulfur
White	Calcite	Calcium
White	Dolomite	Calcium and magnesium
White	Salts	Sodium

The table above shows some of the common causes of soil color in the United States. And while it's true that the average gardener won't much care if her soil contains hematite or lepidocrite, I do think it's handy to know that red or yellow soil is often a sign that there's plenty of iron present. On the other hand, white soil can mean that your soil is rich in calcium or salts, the latter scenario being particularly troublesome since sodium can disrupt your soil structure and can even kill certain plants.

But perhaps the most important clue that soil color gives the gardener is the extent of leaching and waterlogging found in your plot of earth. To understand how water impacts color, you need to know that heavy rainfalls cause water to soak through the upper layers of soil, pulling clay and nutrients down into the subsoil. Over time, the top layer of these weathered soils will become pale while the subsoil becomes dark. This is a sign that you might need to use deep-rooted cover crops to bring important nutrients back up where your vegetables can access them, or you might instead choose to remineralize your soil. I cover both of these techniques in part 3 of this book.

Perennially waterlogged soil turns pale gray and often develops a swampy odor.

Even more problematic is gley—light gray or whitish soil found in waterlogged areas. As with so many soil colors, the root of this gray ground lies with iron, which usually dyes soil particles red or yellow. However, when water fills up all of the spaces between aggregates and blocks out air, microorganisms change both the form and the color of the iron present. In fact, soil iron becomes colorless in the absence of oxygen, which means the natural color of the underlying soil particles—grey or white—can shine through. Meanwhile, anaerobic microorganisms breath out hydrogen sulfide, giving these waterlogged areas their typical swampy odor. Between the smell and the color, it's usually pretty easy to tell which parts of your soil were waterlogged, even if the soil is dry at the moment when you dig.

Similarly, the depth of a gley layer shows the depth of the typically waterlogged ground. For example, if you dig down two and a half feet and don't see any gleying, then you're in pretty good shape. Conversely, light gray soil closer to the surface might harm your crops when the rains return and your plant roots are unable to breathe.

Another possibility is that you'll see mottled patches of light gray and the more natural brown color in a patchwork fashion in your garden earth. In this case, the plot was probably waterlogged for part of the year, but the area drained well enough to allow some iron to regain its color during other portions of the annual cycle.

Although not color-related, since so much of my farm has naturally high groundwater, I have a few more clues I look for to determine whether I need to mound up soil and add drainage to prevent my plants from drowning. Of course, the traditional method of checking soil drainage is to perform a perc test (fill a hole with water and see how fast the liquid drains out), but I prefer more quick-and-dirty hints that also give me a better idea of the long-term water level of that patch of ground.

The obvious clue—a puddle of water that sticks around for days after a heavy rain—is, of course, a definite sign that the soil underneath may be waterlogged. And rushes (grass-like plants with leaves that are round in cross section) or sedges (with leaves triangular in cross section) are another indication that your ground is very wet. If in doubt, I next cut a short line in the sod with my spade and grab the "hair" of the grass to lift it up. If the plants easily peel away from the earth below, holding only an inch or two of dirt within their roots, then the water table is very high and the soil underneath is sure to show pale gray gleying.

Perennially wet soil is a difficult garden problem to deal with, but there are solutions. Flip ahead the chapter 7 if you need more information on drying up wet ground.

Chapter 5: Professional Soil Tests

When It's Time to Pay for a Soil Test

You can test soil at any time of year, but winter is the traditional season.

Depending on how much you enjoy getting muddy, you may be either dismayed or relieved to learn that my suggestions for hands-on soil tests have finally come to a close. Hopefully you discovered that your aggregates are strong, your soil texture is loam, your ground merits an A+ for humus, and your microbes are in tip-top shape. If so, I'll go out on a limb and say that you don't really need a professional soil test. Sure, it might be nice to have that data as a baseline to consider years later, but your garden will likely fare just fine without it.

On the other hand, if your weeds appear to be ailing and your hands-on tests don't provide a clue about the underlying problem, it's time to turn to the pros. I won't go into step-by-step instructions for taking soil samples since each laboratory has slightly different requirements. But I will provide a few tips to make sure you get your money's worth from a professional soil test.

Selecting a Soil-Testing Laboratory

City gardeners are most likely to be concerned about heavy metals in their soil.

My first piece of advice is to choose your lab wisely. And to do so, you'll need to figure out your primary reason for testing your soil in the first place.

I'll start with heavy metals, which have less to do with ailing plants and more to do with concerns about harming your family with homegrown food. You're most likely to be dealing with an accumulation of heavy metals in your soil if you garden in the city, on the site of an old orchard, or near an industrial area—anywhere that chemicals are routinely applied to the air or soil. If that sounds like your garden, then you'll want to make sure the lab you're interested in tests for arsenic, cadmium, copper, lead, nickel, selenium, and zinc. Most don't, so it can take some legwork to track down the proper lab. One of the lowest-cost soil tests that included heavy metals at the time this book was written was provided by UMass Amherst (http://soiltest.umass.edu/services), although other choices may have sprung up in the interim.

While you're assessing your own testing needs, this is also a good time to decide if you're interested in remineralization. The term refers to a method of bringing your garden's micro- and macronutrients back into balance using concentrated amendments, and I'll discuss the specifics in more depth later in this book. But, for now, you should simply ask yourself the question—am I interested in adding chemical fertilizers to my soil as a one-time remineralization fix, or do I want to stick solely to organic amendments for slower nutrient balancing? If remineralization is on the table then you'll be better off finding a testing lab that uses a Mehlich 3 soil analysis since this type of extraction technique makes calculations much easier. Logan Labs (www.loganlabs.com) was the cheapest Mehlich 3 option that I found while researching laboratories for this book.

On the other hand, if you're not specifically interested in either heavy metals or in remineralization, you may find that your state's extension service is the cheapest source for soil testing. Home gardeners often have to pay a nominal fee to utilize this government service, but extension agents usually test farm soil for free. And, as an added bonus, extension-service test results also tend to come with an in-depth analysis that will help you figure out what your results mean, which can really make that big table of numbers that shows up in your inbox less daunting. Visit http://nifa.usda.gov/partners-and-extension-map to find your local extension agent's contact information if you'd like to use these govern-ment-sponsored testing labs.

Understanding Your Test Results

Soil Report

			2	7	8	10	6
Job Name	Anna Hess				Date	1/4/2013	
Company	Anna Hess		Submitted By				
Sample Location			2	7	8	10	6
Sample ID							
Lab Number			38	39	40	41	42
Sample Depth in inches			6	6	6	6	6
Total Exchange Capacity (M. E.)			12.58	10.92	6.20	13.91	7.65
pH of Soil Sample			6.50	7.20	6.30	7.10	5.10
Organic Matter, Percent			8.49	9.95	5.43	6.53	2.74
ANIONS SULFUR:	p.p.m.		20	18	20	16	15
Mehlich III Phosphorous:	as (P$_2$O$_5$) lbs / acre		345	1136	269	778	56
EXCHANGEABLE CATIONS CALCIUM: lbs / acre	Desired Value		3422	2969	1685	3784	2079
	Value Found		3078	2596	1305	3687	894
	Deficit		-344	-373	-380	-97	-1185
MAGNESIUM: lbs / acre	Desired Value		362	314	200	400	220
	Value Found		575	654	261	672	249
	Deficit						
POTASSIUM: lbs / acre	Desired Value		392	340	200	434	238
	Value Found		648	918	592	944	415
	Deficit						
SODIUM:	lbs / acre		46	31	55	41	37
BASE SATURATION % Calcium (60 to 70%)			61.16	59.45	52.66	66.25	29.23
Magnesium (10 to 20%)			19.04	24.96	17.55	20.12	13.57
Potassium (2 to 5%)			6.60	10.78	12.25	8.70	6.96
Sodium (.5 to 3%)			0.80	0.63	1.94	0.63	1.04
Other Bases (Variable)			4.90	4.20	5.10	4.30	7.20
Exchangable Hydrogen (10 to 15%)			7.50	0.00	10.50	0.00	42.00
TRACE ELEMENTS Boron (p.p.m.)			0.44	0.49	< 0.2	0.76	< 0.2
Iron (p.p.m.)			134	215	177	169	92
Manganese (p.p.m.)			56	31	24	56	42
Copper (p.p.m.)			4.71	2.54	2.08	2.57	1.32
Zinc (p.p.m.)			23.09	13.42	4.1	9.73	1.17
Aluminum (p.p.m.)			301	216	327	233	402
OTHER							

At first glance, your soil-test results may appear daunting.

Okay, now you've sent soil off to a lab and the results have come back. What should you look at first?

pH is one of the most common soil issues that the previously listed hands-on tests won't pinpoint. I won't delve into the chemistry of pH here, but every gardener should understand that pH of 7 is considered neutral while soils with a lower pH are acidic (sometimes called "sour") and soils with a higher pH are alkaline (sometimes called "basic" or "sweet").

The perfect pH for most garden soil is slightly acidic, with a pH between 6 and 7. If you're growing blueberries or azaleas, of course, you're looking for much more acidic ground. But usually, a pH below 6 is considered a problem while a pH above 7.5 can also be an issue for your plants. Please turn to chapter 11 for more details on repairing the pH of your soil if this value lies outside the recommended range in your plot of earth.

If you're pretty sure there's a problem with your soil that isn't due to an improper pH, the next spot to look is at your nitrogen and organic matter levels. But that topic deserves its own section (coming up next), so I'll instead point your eyes toward a fourth possibility—extreme mineral imbalances. Most soil reports will list the recommended levels of each nutrient along with the value found in your soil; levels excessively above or excessively below this recommended range can cause problems for your plants. Once again, I'll turn you to chapter 12 if you think nutrient excesses or deficiencies are at the root of your plants' failure to thrive.

That said, in the vast majority of cases, puny plants can be attributed to either too little nitrogen, to improper pH, or to a paucity of organic matter. And, in the end, the first two problems often stem from the same source as the last. So let's delve a little deeper into the slow-but-sure fix to most common soil problems—bringing your organic-matter levels into line.

Organic Matter and Nitrogen

Are you ready for that in-depth description of organic matter that I've been promising you for the last few chapters? I decided to include the information here for three reasons. First, a paucity of organic matter is one of the most likely reasons your garden soil might not be going the distance. Plus, your soil-test results give you the information you need to really understand this interesting topic. Finally, I figure if you're even reading this chapter, you're okay with taking on a bit of math and science. So sit back and prepare to learn much more than you probably ever wanted to know about soil organic matter.

I'll start by telling you that I consider organic-matter levels to be the most important facet of my soil's report card. Why? Because organic matter impacts not only the texture of my soil (as I explained earlier), but also how well plants are able to find the essential nutrients they need in order to grow.

Let's start with nitrogen—that number-one nutrient without which your plants will be puny and their leaves yellow. Unfortunately, nitrogen moves through dirt very quickly, either getting used up by living things or simply washing away during heavy rains. So it can be hard to keep enough nitrogen on hand throughout the growing season . . . unless your organic-matter levels are high.

How does the partnership work? It's simple. The so-called active portion of your organic matter is constantly decomposing to release more nitrogen to feed those hungry roots and microbes, acting like a slow-release fertilizer. So increasing your soil's organic-matter levels is like creating a bank for that all-important soil nutrient.

"Okay," you tell me, "I'm sold. But how much organic matter do I really need? This stuff is heavy and hard to find!" More organic matter is nearly always better, but a good goal is to see a figure of at least 5% organic matter on your soil's report card. At this level, your active organic matter produces

about 100 pounds of available nitrogen per acre per year ...
which just happens to fit the requirements of your average
garden vegetable.

Yellowish leaves on heavy feeders like corn are a classic indicator of
nitrogen deficiency. Here, I'm using two techniques to boost nitrogen
levels in an existing crop. First, I went for a quick fix—pouring on diluted
urine for immediate nutrition. Next, I top-dressed with extra compost
for long-term nitrogen availability. Finally (after this photo was taken), I
covered the amended soil with straw to prevent the compost from drying out. Two weeks later, the corn plants were dark green and tassling
up, and they ended up producing a good quantity of very tasty ears.

Unfortunately, that critical 5% is much easier to achieve in
some parts of the country than in others. For example, if you
live in a hot climate and garden in sandy soil, your organic
matter will break down much faster than if you garden in

clay in New England. So, for southerners, you may have to be happy with as low as 2% organic matter at the end of a long, humid summer.

On the other hand, those New Englanders don't really have it made in the shade. Their active organic matter is less active—meaning it decomposes slower and produces less nitrogen—especially during their long, cold winters and dreary springs. So northerners should aim for even higher organic-matter levels, and they may also need to apply faster-acting sources of nitrogen—such as diluted urine, compost tea, or seed meals—when feeding their spring and fall crops during cool weather.

The heaviest feeders in a typical vegetable garden include sweet corn, tomatoes, squash, and cabbage.

When it comes to supplying nitrogen organically, I like to consider the life of a garden in two phases. First there's the development phase when you're bringing your organic-matter levels up to par. During this period, it's worth integrating large doses of organic matter using tricks like hugelkultur (a.k.a. buried logs—see chapter 17) or extensive cover cropping, and you'll also want to feed your soil as much compost as your back and wallet can handle. I try to apply at least an inch of compost before every planting during the development phase of a garden plot, which may mean I'm laying down up to three inches of compost per year if I grow a three-season garden.

After anywhere from two to ten years, depending on how hard you hit the early organic-matter amendments and how bad your soil was to begin with, you've achieved the maintenance stage. Now your soil reports should be showing at least 5% organic matter, unless you're one of those sandy southerners. At this point, you can finally back off and simply ensure that you're adding as much organic matter as your soil loses to decomposition during a given year. Maintenance levels of compost addition in this scenario are about 2,000 pounds (or one cubic yard) per acre annually to replace what's been broken down to feed your crops. That equates to a very thin dusting of compost over the soil every year.

Since it can be tough to apply such a small amount of compost evenly, an alternative is to follow follow the lead of Jean-Martin Fortier, author of *The Market Gardener*. Fortier only provides compost to his heavy feeders annually, spreading one large wheelbarrow load per 600 square feet around tomatoes, garlic, cucurbits (like squashes), and non-leafy brassicas (like cabbages). Medium feeders (like onions and leafy greens) instead get by on a small dose of poultry manure to keep the nitrogen cycling, while peas and beans are left to grow with no amendments at all. This technique works well as long as you have a well-thought-out garden-rotation program to ensure that each plot is treated to compost at least every other year.

Of course, if your plants don't thrive under this low-amendment regime, chances are you haven't achieved the maintenance phase quite yet. In that case, buckle back down and add more organic matter. It's almost certain to fix what ails you.

Organic Matter and CEC

A phosphorus deficiency often shows up in fruiting sweet corn as purple margins on lower leaves. Another common sign of phosphorus deficiency is purple or red undersides of young tomato leaves. In either case, organic matter is a good solution since humus provides about 60% of an average soil's available phosphorus.

Amending with high-nitrogen fertilizers produces such obvious results that it's easy to think this nutrient is the be-all and end-all of plant nutrition. But plants require many other micro- and macronutrients in smaller doses during the course of growing and making fruit. Luckily, organic matter does just as good of a job of keeping these other nutrients available, even though the specifics are a little bit different.

When it comes to nutrients other than nitrogen, it's handy to look at another number on your soil-test analysis—the cation exchange capacity, sometimes labeled as "CEC" or "total exchange capacity." CEC relates to a second major job of organic matter—to hold onto the nutrients that tend to leach out of soils during heavy rains. And even though CEC technically relates only to positively charged nutrients like calcium, magnesium, and potassium, similar facets of your organic matter that aren't as frequently measured by testing labs also help your dirt hold onto other nutrients like phosphorus as well. So for the sake of our home-garden-scale analysis, you can simply consider CEC to be a measurement of how good a job your organic matter is doing at holding onto nutrients in general.

Just as you should aim for at least 5% organic matter on your test results to ensure optimal nitrogen availability, good soil will also have a cation exchange capacity of at least 11 mEq/100 g. Unfortunately, this level can be harder to achieve than straight percentage of organic matter since CEC is influenced largely by what's sometimes called passive organic matter but which gardeners will recognize as really high-class compost—that hard-to-find humus we think of as black gold.

What's the difference between active and passive organic matter? The clue lies in the name. Active organic matter, as I mentioned earlier, breaks down readily to provide plant nutrients, while passive organic matter tends to stay put in your soil for hundreds or even thousands of years.

Humus begins as tough-to-decompose organic matter like wood and tree leaves, which are broken down into humic acids by fungi and actinomycetes.

The sources of these different types of organic matter vary too. Active organic matter tends to start out as the "greens" in compost—as sugars, starches, and proteins—which are then decomposed by bacteria into falvic acids. Passive organic matter, in contrast, begins as cellulose and lignin (the "browns"), which are converted into humic acids by the action of fungi and actinomycetes.

You may recall from the last section that the active portion of your organic matter is what decomposes to produce nitrogen and other nutrients for your crops. And since active organic matter feeds microbes as well as plants, this component of soil is essential for the production of aggregates that create good soil texture too.

Passive organic matter, on the other hand, is equally valuable because it latches onto leachable nutrients and is responsible for much of your soil's CEC. As a result, the easiest way to improve your soil's ability to hold onto plant-friendly nutrients is to add well-composted organic matter that began life as relatively woody debris. Another alternative for improving your passive-organic-matter levels is to grow tough-stemmed cover crops like rye that create humus in situ.

Hopefully that long description was inspiring rather than daunting. And now for the good news—your chemistry lesson is over and it's time to get back to the hands-on portion of this book!

PART 2

SMALL-SCALE NO-TILL GARDENING BASICS

This part of our garden was once home to such poor soil that even cover crops failed to thrive. But years of no-till management were sufficient to turn the plot into a vibrant growing zone. In 2015, the area pictured produced a dozen large cabbages, five bushels of tomatoes, a bushel of sweet potatoes, and 225 pounds of butternut squash. Not bad for soggy soil with all of the topsoil eroded away.

As you've probably already gathered, one of the primary interests of a soil-friendly gardener should be organic-matter levels. In my case, that obsession inevitably led me toward no-till gardening.

What's the big deal with no-till? One study followed twenty-three years of growing successive crops of chemically-fertilized corn with no soil-building in between, with half the fields using traditional tillage and the other half using no-till technology. The scientists found that—even without the benefit of organic amendments like compost and mulch—the no-till fields contained six times as much organic matter at the end of the study compared to the conventionally plowed fields. You can think of that result as the worst-case scenario of no-till gardening, since you'll hopefully be using compost, mulch, and cover crops to boost your organic matter levels in addition to no-till strategies. Wouldn't it be interesting to see how the combination of organic fertilization with no-till methodology could exponentially increase the benefits of ever increasing organic-matter levels?

No-till farming can sometimes sound like magic, but the results make sense once you realize you're turning back the clock on the negative effects of plowing. The trouble is that both plowing and tilling lower organic-matter levels dramatically, in part because excessive aeration burns through the banked organic matter in record time. Other studies have shown that tilling breaks down soil structure and removes biopores; that tilling lowers water infiltration, aeration, and root-growth rates; and that churning up the soil snuffs out beneficial fungi known as mycorrhizae that help roots find nutrients.

To cut a long story short—your rototiller is bad for your dirt. In fact, the home tiller is even worse for soil structure than the average plow. So if I don't manage to sell you on no-till methodology by the end of this book, you might at least choose to hire out your soil-processing step to someone with a tractor in an effort to reduce your tillage to the bare minimum.

No-till soil isn't as light and fluffy as recently tilled ground, but the stable soil aggregates make it easy for roots, air, and water to move through the untilled earth.

If tilling is so deadly, then why do we till? Plowing or tilling *does* improve soil structure initially by creating a loose seedbed through which baby plants can easily spread their roots. Tilling helps soil dry out more quickly after rains, which means the earth warms up faster in the spring (but also cools down faster in the fall). And tilling is an essential tool in the farmer's arsenal when battling weeds. In fact, I'd hesitate to recommend the techniques involved in mainstream no-till agriculture to anyone since large-scale farmers replace the tilling step with herbicide usage in an effort to keep unwanted weed seedlings at bay.

Luckily, as a home gardener, you can enjoy all of the benefits of no-till gardening while suffering through few of the pitfalls. So for the next few chapters I'll explain the techniques I use to start new no-till beds and then to manage them through years of quality vegetable production . . . all without ever firing up the rototiller. Once you realize how easy these methods are, perhaps you'll also consider giving the soil-friendly technique a try.

Chapter 6: Two Ways to Start a No-Till Garden

Kill Mulches

"I'm sold!" you tell me. "But how do I start?" The best method for transforming a patch of sod into a no-till garden will depend on how patient you are and on your soil's initial quality. I'll suggest some alternative techniques later for those of you starting with poor ground, but in the meantime let's take a look at my old standby—the kill mulch (also known as a lasagna garden or sheet mulch).

Kill mulches make the most sense if your soil is relatively loose (rather than compacted), if the plants currently growing in the area aren't too ornery (grass is easy to kill, blackberries not so much), and if your water situation is neither swampy nor bone dry. This is the purest way to start a no-till garden since you won't burn up any organic matter and won't dismantle the soil structure in the process. However, a kill mulch requires more time between starting and planting than some of the other methods I'll mention later, and it also has the potential to cause problems if your ground isn't quite up to par. So I recommend using kill mulches with a bit of caution.

Those caveats aside, kill mulches make a lot of sense in the backyard because they're easy, they require few (or no) tools, and the requisite supplies can often be found in your friendly neighborhood dumpster. To begin, I run a lawn mower over the ground to cut the existing vegetation as close to the soil surface as possible, or I simply pull a chicken tractor over the spot to knock down tall weeds. Either way, I leave grass clippings or other organic matter to lie where they fall unless the plants are extremely seedy since the debris will add more biomass to my soil. Then I move on to the next layer.

At its simplest, a kill mulch consists of a layer of overlapping cardboard sheets . . .

. . . covered with a layer of straw. This type of kill mulch can be planted into several months later.

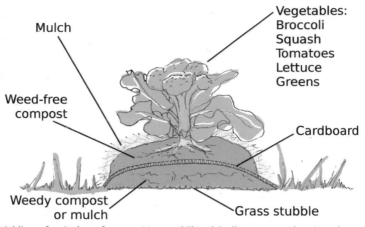

Mulch

Vegetables:
Broccoli
Squash
Tomatoes
Lettuce
Greens

Weed-free
compost

Cardboard

Weedy compost
or mulch

Grass stubble

Adding a few inches of compost to your kill mulch allows you to plant into the new garden area immediately.

If you have any on hand, you can lay down weedy mulch or manure as the next (optional) layer. Personally, I never have biomass available that isn't already earmarked for another project, but if you're less greedy with your biomass, this is a good use for grass clippings that contain seed heads or spoiled hay and bedding from an animal barn where fodder has fallen onto the floor. It's safe to apply these weed sources deep in the kill mulch since you won't ever be churning up the garden's soil with a tiller, so any seeds will simply lie in the earth until they rot down into compost.

Whether or not you apply weedy mulch or manure, the next layer of your kill mulch consists of cardboard or newspaper meant to block existing vegetation from growing back up to the surface. In my opinion, corrugated cardboard is vastly superior to paper in this application. Since the former material contains glues that are very tasty to soil microorganisms, it seems to block weeds better, and it also (counterintuitively) rots faster than paper. However, if all you've got is newspaper, by all means use it . . . as long as the paper isn't glossy or embedded with too many colored dyes. (See chapter 17 for an in-depth discussion of using paper and cardboard in the garden.)

Either way, you'll want to decide whether to soak the paper or cardboard before application. This step is essential in arid climates or during droughts and it's also handy for preventing newspaper from flying away during application. In fact, if your climate is extremely dry, you should also take the time to thoroughly saturate the soil before laying down any cardboard or paper since a new kill mulch will tend to shed rainwater for the first few weeks after being built. Luckily, the new beds will also hold onto any moisture laid down beneath the mulch layers, so a good watering at the start can go a long way.

On the other hand, if you live in a wet climate like I do, you can simply lay down dry sheets of cardboard or newspaper to create your kill layer. Occasionally I need to mold cardboard across an irregular soil surface, in which case I may leave the material out in the rain for a day or two beforehand to pre-hydrate. But, otherwise, I simply count on our natural inch of rain per week to naturally moisten my kill mulches.

When you're ready to actually put the kill layer in place, pick a day when there's no wind in the forecast since your hard work can quickly blow away otherwise. Now, lay down one sheet of cardboard or about six to ten sheets of newspaper at a time, overlapping each edge by at least two inches so wily weeds can't poke through the cracks.

This thickness is sufficient to kill off grasses and most weeds that you'll find in an average lawn, but a less maintained area calls for double that thickness. In the photos at the top of this section, for example, I've kept my flattened boxes doubled up (meaning that I didn't tear apart the glued seam that would let me separate them out into one longer, thinner sheet of cardboard) since the area in question had only been reclaimed from blackberries and honeysuckle for one mowing season. In contrast, I usually lay down single sheets of cardboard over grassy lawns since the more frugal use of materials allows me to cover twice the area with the same amount of cardboard.

A couple of months after construction, this kill mulch has done its job—all of the grasses underneath have perished.

In a perfect world, I would build kill mulches in the fall or early winter for spring planting, and in late winter to early spring for late summer or fall planting. But, as you may have already realized, I'm an impatient gardener and I often want to plant into kill mulches *now*. If you're also in a hurry, you'll want to rustle up several inches of compost and/or weed-free topsoil to lay down on top of the kill mulch I've thus far described. Using this technique, you'll be able to plant directly into the kill mulch immediately, especially if you focus on relatively shallow-rooted vegetables that thrive in high-organic-matter soils. I would never plant carrots or sweet potatoes directly into a young kill mulch, but crucifers like broccoli and cabbage, cucurbits like cucumbers and squash, leafy greens like lettuce and kale, and even tomatoes often do well in newly kill mulched beds as long as you keep the nitrogen levels high.

If you don't need bare soil to direct-seed into, the final layer of the kill mulch is the actual mulch material, preferably straw if you're making a new bed for vegetables or wood chips or tree leaves if you're making a new bed for woody plants. In other words, at its simplest, a kill mulch can simply consist of a layer of cardboard topped off with some straw to weigh the weed-control layer down. Then you would wait a few months before raking back the straw, throwing down an inch of compost, and enjoying a no-till garden bed that comes with perfect soil structure and that was created with minimal work.

Tilling Up a No-Till Bed

The title of this section sounds like an oxymoron, but the technique is a perfectly acceptable way to start a no-till garden if you're in a hurry or have major soil problems to deal with before planting. Yes, tilling the soil before planting for the first time will wreak havoc on your soil ecosystem. But once you stop mixing the earth around, things will come back into balance pretty quickly. And, on the plus side, a tilled bed is ready to plant into nearly immediately, while also giving you the opportunity to deal with waterlogging, compaction, and problematic nutrient levels. So if your soil is extremely troubled, it might be worth taking one step back in preparation for two steps forward.

I actually used the tillage method to begin the majority of my current vegetable garden before I'd heard of the term no-till, so I can tell you from firsthand experience how it works. First, I stood over my husband as he operated the rototiller, making sure that he was only churning up the topsoil (the dark layer near the surface) rather than mixing in the subsoil (the paler layer underneath). Next, I determined where my permanent beds were going to go and how wide my aisles were going to be. (See *The Weekend Homesteader* for more details on bed planning.) And, finally, I scooped the topsoil out of the aisles and onto the beds. The result is a double layer of topsoil in the garden beds, while the aisles can either be permanently mulched or can be mowed and allowed to turn into sod.

In the photo above, taken in March 2007, my husband is tilling new ground and I've recently shoveled up topsoil to create raised beds. Several methods showcased here fell by the wayside in later years. The white paper in the aisles (free roll ends from a printer) proved to be more trouble than it was worth, as were the log borders. In addition, I learned the hard way that it's much easier to manage long beds with relatively wide aisles rather than the patchwork quilt of smaller beds and narrow aisles that are shown here. However, the basic method of mounding up the topsoil out of the aisles to form permanent raised beds has gone the distance. With no compaction treatment other than cover crops, this soil is still prime growing area nine years later.

Here's the same garden three months after construction, in June 2007.

As you can tell, building these beds requires more work than laying down a kill mulch, but the tillage-and-mounding step is something you only need to do once during the lifetime of a garden. Since permanent garden beds make the most sense in a no-till plot, after this first step you can sell your rototiller and move on to the no-till maintenance techniques I outline in chapter 9.

Chapter 7: Correcting Soil Problems as You Build New Beds

Too Wet or Too Dry

The doubled-topsoil technique outlined in the last chapter worked perfectly in parts of my garden, but I'd tweak the design if my climate or soil had inherent limitations. For example, if I lived in an area with sandy soil and a dry climate, then mounding up the topsoil to make raised beds would be problematic since the technique would exacerbate the existing lack of moisture. Instead, I might choose to excavate some of the subsoil from the garden-bed areas and use it elsewhere, then I'd pour all of the topsoil from both the bed and aisles into the hole to create a sunken pit garden that would retain moisture and would keep plant roots close to the groundwater.

If your terrain isn't entirely flat, you can build these sunken beds on contour (perpendicular to the slope), which will allow the pits to hold onto any water that flows over the ground during heavy rainfall events. In this case, your beds have become swales, and it might be safer to plant your vegetables on the wall that rises up out of the downhill side of the swale rather than on the very bottom of the pit. Alternatively, you can add a drainage ditch to your arrangement and block the entrance with a piece of wood as a low-tech method of keeping the water in the pit during dry spells then easily channeling deluges away when rains eventually fall.

Pit gardens are a traditional technique used by Native Americans in the American Southwest, so they are definitely more than a book gardener's brainchild. That said, once you see the pictures of the swamp in which I garden, you'll quickly realize that I haven't tried out any pit gardens personally. So please take my explanation with a grain of salt and start small when experimenting with this method in your own sandy soil. Or, if you'd rather be safe rather than sorry, stick to hugelkultur (explained in depth in chapter 17) to increase your soil's moisture-retentive properties without risking winter floods.

If you pick a dry period to dig into waterlogged ground, you can simply excavate the aisles until you hit standing water, then rake the mostly-dry soil flat on top of the newly raised bed. Digging should be easy since roots can't reach far into water-logged ground. (As a side note, the strange, tarp-wrapped bundle on the right side of this photo is a Chicago Hardy fig, which is only able to withstand zone-6 winters with the help of some freeze protection.)

On the other hand, you might be dealing with the same problem I have in parts of my garden—a very high water table combined with a wet climate that means plant roots habitually drown. In this case, it's worth digging some of the subsoil out of the aisles and mounding up both subsoil and all of the topsoil to create new garden beds that are quite a bit taller than you might otherwise build.

Two months after mounding up soil, tomatoes were thriving in the new ground and a tree frog moved in to lay her eggs in the standing water of the aisles.

In this case, I recommend using elbow grease alone for soil preparation since tilling wet soil completely dismantles the soil structure. Instead, simply shovel clumps of sod out of the aisles, laying each mass upside down atop the existing grass in the area where your new garden bed will lie. As you work, pull out roots of problematic weeds like burdock, thistles, and Japanese honeysuckle, but leave most of the plant matter in place to decompose within the new bed.

After you've moved all of the topsoil to the new garden bed, the next step is to shovel on enough subsoil so that your bed's final surface is raised out of the water-danger zone. Next, rake apart any clumps, then lay down a kill mulch as best you can. Newspaper is the optimal weed-control layer in this instance since the wet paper will mold well to irregularly shaped beds. No matter what kill layer you use, you'll need to plan on a few months of mellowing time to kill the former sod, and you may also need to refresh your kill mulch a few times in the interim to produce a weed-free planting zone.

A final factor to consider before I turn you loose with your shovel is orientation. If you're building a new raised bed to deal with waterlogged soil, you should be sure to plan ahead for drainage. Perhaps you want to build very high raised beds on contour the way you'd manage swales so you won't need to irrigate at all during the summer months, a technique that is based on Central American chinampas and that is pictured on the preceding pages. Alternatively, perhaps you'd rather build your raised beds parallel to the slope so that excess water drains away.

I've used the chinampa technique with good results for summer vegetables (with the caveat that I have to weed while wearing galoshes) and the latter technique with good results for perennials (who would drown in our winter swamp if water wasn't prompted to flow away from their root zone during the wet season). In the latter scenario, you may also want to use drainage tiles (perforated plastic pipes) to move subsurface water out of the garden. But keep in mind that these pipes will likely need maintenance over time and that you'll need to do something with the excess water. Perhaps a downstream pond is the solution?

Other Common Soil Issues

Moving on from my pet subject of waterlogged ground, there are a few other soil problems you might want to correct at the same time you build a new bed. Compaction is an obvious issue since most city soils and worn-out farmland will have a hardpan layer that makes it difficult for air and water to percolate deep into the subsoil. I wrote about several ways to prevent and fix compaction in chapter 2, so here I'll just mention additional techniques often used in the early stages of creating a new garden plot. Double-digging essentially consists of removing all of the topsoil, breaking up the subsoil (either by tilling, shoveling, or fluffing it up with a broadfork), then putting the topsoil back in place. If you're farming on a larger scale and have access to heavy machinery, then a chisel plow can do the same job without breaking your back.

Broadforks break apart compaction without mixing up the soil layers. You can read more about how to choose and use broadforks in chapter 9.

While we're talking about urban soils, I should mention that city gardeners deal with several unique problems not usually faced by those of us who farm in more rural settings. In addition to compaction, you might find chunks of buried concrete that dramatically increase your soil's pH. In addition, heavy metals and other such materials are common contaminants. Finally, urban soils tend to be hot due to their proximity to pavement, and the populations of beneficial fungi known as mycorrhizae are generally low. Many of these issues can be fixed by incorporating massive amounts of organic matter, and sometimes urban growers also choose to create new raised beds entirely from scratch using trucked-in topsoil/compost mixtures. Remember—it's worth putting some extra elbow grease into the early stages of garden preparation if the time and money means safer and more delicious harvests for the entire life of your garden.

I mentioned pH in relation to city gardens above, but you should be aware that excessively acidic or alkaline soil can be found in any part of the world. No matter where you live, it's worth checking your soil test results, reading chapters 11 and 12, then mixing the necessary amendments to fix pH and mineral imbalances into the topsoil as you make a new garden bed. And if you live in an arid area where rainfall is minimal and where salts tend to build up in soil, consider leaching excess sodium away using heavy irrigation if your test results suggest that salty soil is a problem.

Chapter 8: Solarization

*Faster, Easier Ways to Start a
New No-Till Bed*

In 2015, I tried out four experimental techniques of starting no-till garden beds in a month or less. Only one method really made the cut.

In chapter 6, I outlined two techniques of starting a no-till garden bed from scratch, but each has a major disadvantage. Kill mulches either require the input of lots of compost or a several month wait, while tilled beds dismantle your soil structure and can be hard on your back. So in spring of 2015 I gave myself a challenge—I wanted to find a technique that would allow me to plant into a very weedy garden area after one month or less with very little work.

Before I delve into the successes and failures in this department, I want to back up and start with a big warning. This chapter is really most relevant to folks who have an existing garden plot in which the soil is in relatively good shape but where neglect has allowed weeds to take over. For example, say you'd never heard of no-till last fall, so you rototilled, planted a big spring garden, then just ignored the plot as grasses and clovers started outcompeting your tomatoes and squash in late summer and early fall. That scenario is the perfect fit for the methods outlined in this section.

I'll start with the techniques that didn't really make the cut. Garden-supply companies are now selling very thin, biodegradable black plastic (pictured covering the front bed in the photo on the previous page) along with so-called paper mulches (pictured covering the second bed from the front in the photo on the previous page). Having tried both products, I wouldn't recommend them except as a weed-control layer post-tilling or post-weeding in an established garden plot. I made the mistake of applying these barriers in weedier ground, and plants (with the help of my cat) poked holes in both the plastic and the paper before weeds could be smothered by these thin sheets.

The third and fourth rows from the front in my photo are a modification of my run-of-the-mill kill mulch. I laid down overlapping layers of newspaper then weighed that kill layer down with manurey bedding straight from our goat barn. This row did exactly as I expected—the light-blocking newspaper pretty much killed the weeds within a month, but the paper didn't degrade very quickly, which made planting into the bed a chore. Plus, some of the newspapers blew away, which cluttered up the yard and left weedy areas within the row

The final bed in the photo on the previous page showcases the winning technique—solarization. Basically, solarization consists of using clear plastic to create a greenhouse effect that cooks the weeds underneath during a very short span of time. To tell you the truth, I was leery of solarization from the get-go, worrying that the high temperatures would also destroy my beloved soil microorganisms. But as you'll soon see, the technique quickly became one of my favorite methods of not only starting a new no-till garden bed, but also of solving weed problems that I let get out of hand later in the gardening year.

Solarization Basics

Solarization consists of laying down a sheet of clear plastic, then waiting two weeks for the weeds underneath to cook.

I'll tell you up front that solarization is a summery, southern trick. Simply covering the ground with a thin sheet of clear plastic killed 99% of annual and shallow-rooted weeds in my garden in a mere two weeks . . . as long as the days were reliably hitting 90 degrees, there were few clouds in the sky, and the area was exposed to full sunlight. Add in partial shade from trees or extended cloudy weather, though, and solarization failed to do the trick. In addition, deep-rooted perennial weeds survived beneath my solarization plastic, and the northern sides of high raised beds also provided too much shade to reliably kill all of the annual weeds. So you should be aware that this technique has some relatively extreme limitations before you plan on solarization healing all of your weeding woes.

That said, during hot summer days, solarization worked like magic. My husband bought me a relatively heavy plastic drop cloth, and the cheap covering lasted all summer, renovating multiple garden areas in quick succession. In fact, I probably could have used the same plastic for a second summer if I hadn't allowed holes to be poked in the sheet when I tried to solarize an area with very woody weeds. On the other hand, if you're not keen on buying new plastic just for solarization, one of our blog readers suggested that greenhouse film could be moved into solarization duty once the plastic is no longer quite strong enough to hold together around hoop-house frames.

No matter where you find your clear plastic, first mow down any tall weeds as if you were preparing for a kill mulch. Next, spread the plastic over top and weigh down the edges and the middle so the sheet comes in close contact with the earth. I used rebar for weights since I had some on hand, but plenty of alternatives exist. Your weights could be rocks, dirt, or anything else as long as you add enough to make sure the plastic doesn't blow away during heavy winds. It's also important to ensure that the edges of the sheet don't ruck up and allow hot air to leak out, diluting your solarization effect.

Solarization is very effective at killing annuals and shallow-rooted perennials. The soybeans in this photo are shown a couple of weeks after planting into a newly solarized bed.

After your solarization film is in place, wait until all of the green goes away, then peel back your plastic and plant. As with any gardening technique, the proof is in the pudding—and solarization pudding is much better than I expected. In fact, I was surprised to find that my solarized beds seemed to have more worms than could be found beneath recent kill mulches, probably because the plant matter was more thoroughly decomposed under the clear plastic. Similarly, my experiments with planting directly into solarized beds found seedling survival rates to be higher than in kill mulched beds, although in this case I suspect the benefit was from fewer slugs and cutworms eating up seedlings before they could really get growing. In the end, I had to admit that my gut reaction had been dead wrong—solarization seems to keep my soil ecosystem happy rather than causing any long-term harm.

When everything was said and done, I found only one major disadvantage of solarized beds—dryness during the peak of summer. Since plastic blocks out rain, you may be surprised by how parched the soil gets after just a couple of weeks under cover. Luckily, this disadvantage is easy to fix. Just water your seeds well if you want them to grow right away, or wait for a rain and enjoy watching your solarized ground come back to life.

Clear Plastic versus Black Plastic

When I first wrote about my solarization experiments on my blog, I noticed that many readers had a very hard time working their heads around the differing purposes of black and clear plastic. Just in case you're similarly confused, I thought it was worth delving a little deeper into this topic here.

At the beginning of this chapter, I mentioned not being impressed by thin sheets of biodegradable black plastic. In contrast, the heftier version that's woven to allow air and water to pass through while resisting several years' worth of ultraviolet rays has more utility in the no-till garden. This type of black plastic basically acts like a newspaper or cardboard kill layer, blocking light so weeds underneath die from lack of energy but not requiring reapplication every few months like the paper products do. As a result, heavy layers of black plastic are appropriate for long-term use as weed-control around perennials, or for short-term use as a kill mulch to prepare new garden beds. That said, you shouldn't expect black plastic to kill the weeds underneath as quickly as clear plastic in the summer since the former starves the weeds while the latter cooks them.

Another potential use for black plastic in a no-till garden is occultation. This method, which began in Europe but has since been popularized in the US by Jean-Martin Fortier, consists of preparing your seed bed, then laying down a sheet of black plastic for two to four weeks prior to planting. The plastic heats the soil and sprouts weed seeds therein, then kills those germinated weeds by blocking their access to sunlight. The result is much lower weed pressure after you remove the plastic and plant your vegetables into the bare ground.

Non-biodegradable black plastic works differently from clear plastic, but both have a place in the no-till garden.

I hope this elaboration helps you decide whether you want to use black or clear plastic in your garden. In the end, you might choose to invest in a little bit of both so you can try out all of the different tricks that simplify modern gardening life. Yes, plastic is made from petrochemicals and will eventually end up in the landfill. But if you can grow twice as much food with it compared to without it, then the environmental effects might be a win-win.

Chapter 9: No-Till Garden Management

Weed Control in a No-Till Garden

This photo illustrates three no-till weed-control techniques. In the foreground, you can see that I've seeded my lettuce so thickly that leaves touch when plants are only a few weeks old, shading out sun-loving weeds. Meanwhile, I've mulched the edges of the beds with straw to keep grass and clover from running up out of the aisles. Finally, rye is growing in the background in a fallow garden space, building organic matter while ensuring that no weeds will gain a toehold during the off season.

Once a no-till garden bed is in place, growing food in that space isn't terribly different from planting vegetables in a traditional garden. Beyond the obvious disparity of tilling or not tilling, in fact, the major differences between traditional and no-till gardening revolve around keeping weeds at bay.

The anti-weeding campaign is best started at planting time, when no-till gardeners may choose to space vegetables much closer together than is recommended on the seed packet. In my own garden, I often broadcast small-seeded vegetables like carrots, lettuce, and kale by filling my hand with seeds, spreading my fingers very slightly apart, then giving my arm a little shake to dust seeds across the bed surface. Yes, this results in planting densities much higher than recommended, but the vegetables soon fill in all of the gaps between plants, leaving weeds with no light in which to grow.

Using this technique, I can usually hand-weed a bed once when the vegetable seedlings are only a few weeks old, then largely ignore the planting until harvest time. For lettuce and leafy greens, that harvest begins as early as a month after planting, when I give plants a "haircut," harvesting leaves repeatedly in a cut-and-come-again fashion. In contrast, carrots will need a bit more space to fully mature their roots, so I start thinning a month or so after planting, eating the smallest carrots so the remainder have room to continue bulking up.

Transplanting eliminates the need for bare soil in the garden.

Larger vegetables tend to be less keen on the close-planting approach since tomatoes and beans, for example, won't produce well if they lack adequate elbow room. Here, my preemptive weed control takes the form of using homegrown transplants (if possible) and filling the bare soil between young sets with heavy mulches. It's true that transplanting requires a bit more work up front, but the technique can completely eliminate that bare-soil stage that weeds like so much while also jump-starting the spring garden season. To get these benefits, I always transplant tomatoes, peppers, broccoli, cabbage, and brussels sprouts, while other gardeners may choose to raise indoor seedlings of everything from cucurbits to sweet corn.

Winter squash do a pretty good job of keeping weeds at bay once the vines fully cover the soil. But it's handy to give the crop a head start by laying down newspaper covered by straw between "hills" (planting spots) at the same time you insert seeds into the ground.

A simple layer of straw does the trick between medium-sized vegetables like broccoli, but more widely spaced plants respond well to a set-it-and-forget-it mulch consisting of a couple of sheets of newspaper beneath the straw. With this technique, I'm essentially creating a kill mulch everywhere except right where the vegetable plants poke through the soil surface, so it's necessary to water well before laying down newspapers if your ground is dry. Adding newspapers to my mulching campaign lowered my workload dramatically in 2015 and was particularly effective around wide-ranging butternut squash, between rows of sweet corn, and around the bases of tomato plants.

Another important facet of no-till weed-control is to use cover crops to keep the ground shaded and the soil busy during fallow periods between vegetable-planting times. I'll tell you more about my favorite cover crops in chapter 13. For now, suffice it to say that scattering buckwheat seeds after harvesting spring crops like garlic is a great way to ensure the ground is nearly weed-free when the time comes to plant your fall greens. Cover crops also make an excellent ground cover between small trees and berry bushes in the early years when these plants haven't yet filled out their rows.

What if the weeds get away from you after all? First of all, it happens to all of us, so don't beat yourself up. But also don't turn your back on the area and let the weeds go to seed if you can help it. That old saying "One year's weed is seven year's seed" is very true. So instead of ignoring the trouble zone, I recommend treating the weedy area like a new garden bed and using a kill mulch or solarization to bring the weeds back into line as quickly as possible. It's amazing what a little hand-weeding around the base of your favorite plants followed by a few sheets of cardboard can do in terms of making those weed problems go away.

Finally, I feel obliged to mention that market-scale gardeners will likely choose to include different techniques in their weed-control campaigns. Unfortunately, the heavy mulches and extensive hand-weeding that I recommend for the home gardener simply require too much time and money to be effective on scales above about half an acre. In the market-gardener scenario, you might instead turn to flame weeders or long-term plastic mulches to keep weeds at bay, or you may have to bite the bullet and accept a limited amount of tilling.

Growing Vegetables in Poor Soil

I don't usually recommend raising root vegetables in shallow soil, but garlic, radishes, and onions are an exception to the rule.

Weeds are probably the largest deterrent to no-till gardening, but the gardener will inevitably have to contend with other issues as well. Most notably, no-till techniques are slower (if surer) than conventional soil preparation at creating plant-friendly earth in poor ground. That means you may be faced with subpar dirt in certain parts of your garden during the first year or two while you're waiting for the earthworms to do your job. Which begs the question—which edibles can be successfully grown in extremely poor soil?

Had Tolstoy been a gardener, he would have warned that all happy soils are alike, but that each unhappy soil is unhappy in its own unique way. So I can't give you a one-size-fits-all list of vegetables that thrive in troubled ground. That said, if you've already used the tests in the first quarter of this book to figure out why your soil is ailing, you can likely select a vegetable that will fare well even under those specific poor conditions.

Let's start with shallow soil. This issue could be due to compaction in the subsoil, to a high water table, or to a newly applied kill mulch with only a few inches of compost on top. Although I don't usually recommend planting root crops in soils of limited depth, a few root vegetables are actually good choices in this scenario. Specifically, onions, garlic, and radishes are reported to keep their feeder roots closer to the surface than most other vegetables do, so the trio are good growing choices in shallow ground. In contrast deep-rooters like beets, carrots, Swiss chard, parsnips, and winter squash should definitely be avoided in these scenarios.

How about low-nitrogen conditions? This is one of the most common soil problems in new organic gardens since biological sources of nitrogen often take time to release nutrients into the soil. Nitrogen-fixing vegetables—primarily peas and beans—are the obvious choice in this type of poor plot since these vegetables literally create nitrogen out of thin air. Otherwise, it's easier to tell you what *not* to grow. Vegetables with above-average nitrogen demands include potatoes, onions, cabbages, sweet corn, tomatoes, and celery. I recommend steering clear of these heavy feeders if you don't have enough nitrogen to go around and aren't able to pile on the compost.

Another common issue involves poor soil structure. For example, the high raised beds I build in swampy parts of my homestead to pull vegetable roots out of wet soil often end up with clayey subsoil on the surface and with partially decomposing sod in the center. Although these beds mellow into rich growing ground eventually, the first year or two are rough since the heavy soil hinders seedling germination and root growth. Two crops that have thrived for me in this troubled soil are sweet potatoes and sunflowers. In contrast, carrots and butternut squash did so poorly in this type of ground that I might as well have skipped planting entirely. Medium-producers include large-seeded vegetables like beans and corn that can handle heavier soil textures as long as I increase compost applications to boost nitrogen levels for the latter.

Sweet potatoes thrive in certain types of ailing soil. In this photo, the tubers in the basket were harvested from the same square footage as the tubers stacked nearby, but the larger mess of taters came from poorer ground.

Improper pH is another issue that often takes a few years resolve. Luckily, it's relatively easy to select vegetables that do well in excessively acidic or excessively alkaline soil. Carrots, cucumbers, eggplants, green beans, parsnips, peppers, potatoes, sweet corn, tomatoes, watermelon, and winter squash can handle sour soil with a pH as low as 5.5. In contrast, beets, cabbages, cantaloupe, peas, pumpkins, spinach, sweet corn, and tomatoes will grow in alkaline soil with a pH up to 7.5. Outside those ranges, though, you'll be better off sticking to blueberries (acidic soil) or certain ornamentals (alkaline soil).

All of these selections aside, you'll get even better results if you spend a year or two growing cover crops in that recalcitrant part of the garden. Soil-building species like buckwheat and rye will not only add organic matter to your earth, they'll also often go a long way toward fixing the underlying issues that are keeping vegetables from thriving in the first place. For example, soybeans are a great cover crop for very low-nitrogen soil, oats thrive in waterlogged ground, and oilseed radishes are top-notch at both breaking up hardpan and making phosphorus more available near the soil surface. Skip ahead to chapter 13 if you'd like to learn more about integrating these soil-improving crops into your no-till garden.

No-Till Tools

A broadfork is useful in the early stages of creating a kill mulch in compacted ground.

We've dealt with weeds and troubled soil, which leaves one final question for the new gardener—what kind of tools do you need to manage your no-till plot? I'm not going to bore you with a recital of how to use a spade or a trowel in this section, but there *are* a few relatively unique tools that are handy to have around when working with a no-till garden. I'll start with one I've mentioned previously—the broadfork.

Broadforks basically consist of several long, metal spikes that you push into the soil using the weight of your body, then tilt to create furrows without turning over the earth. In other words—you till without tilling, relieving soil compaction and gently fluffing up the ground, but never going so far that you disturb the critters living therein.

Broadforks are fun to use and they definitely relieve the winter doldrums, letting gardeners play in the dirt when the ground would freeze their fingertips. More seriously, I find the tool invaluable in the early stages of kill-mulch construction in areas that have been frequently walked across. Here, earthworms will have a hard time getting up to your compost and mulch offerings, so it's best to bust up the compacted ground to give them a head start.

That said, if your soil is already in good shape due to copious amendments of organic matter and the strict refusal to allow anyone heavier than your cat to walk on the garden beds, you might not need a broadfork at all. How can I say this with such assurance? Because I ran a side-by-side trial to test out this supposition in my own garden, of course. I started out by broadforking half of a bed and leaving the other half untouched. Next, I planted carrot seeds and then paid attention when I harvested both beds a few months later. Yields and straightness were the same for both halves of the test bed, with the only real difference being that carrots in the broadforked half were a little bit easier to harvest using the tug-on-the-top technique. Overall, though, the experience proved to me that I don't really need to use a broadfork as a matter of course in my established garden beds.

On the other hand, if you have severely compacted soil that needs improving, you'll want to splurge on a sturdy broadfork like the ones offered by Meadow Creature (www.meadowcreature.com). Quality is important here since the job of the broadfork is to push its way through rock-hard soil and you don't want the metal tines to bend under pressure. It's also essential to choose a broadfork that's the right size for you and for your garden. Twelve-inch tines are appropriate for those of us who are five foot, four inches or shorter, fourteen-inch models are good for taller gardeners, and sixteen-inch models are really only appropriate for professional farmers.

Hand tools like this Austrian scythe are sufficient to keep a no-till garden in order.

Beyond the broadfork, I primarily use tools that the average gardener likely already has in her arsenal—a wheelbarrow, a spade, a metal rake, a hoe (I prefer the triangular Warren hoe), and a trowel (I prefer the trake—half trowel, half rake). I occasionally use a scythe as well, although I'll admit that I'm lazy enough to instead ask my husband to rev up the Weed Eater during the peak of gardening season. For our grassy garden aisles, we also push a power lawn mower to keep grasses in check.

But, to me, the beauty of a no-till garden lies in how few tools you really need to get the job done. You don't have to buy a tractor, a rototiller, or any other piece of motorized equipment that will break down just when you need it most. Instead, the techniques described in this book keep the ground so soft and healthy that you barely need more than a digging stick to seat your seeds. That's no-till simplicity at its best!

Chapter 10: Beyond the In-Earth Garden

Containers

Self-watering pots like the ones shown above make vegetable gardening in containers much simpler.

Photo credit: Heather Walsh

Before I leave the growing-techniques portion of this book behind, I'd be remiss if I didn't mention a completely different type of gardening—planting vegetables in containers. While the methods I outline in this book will create great soil for your in-the-ground garden, the same soil in a pot turns into compacted, measly dirt. Don't try to grow anything in that—you'll regret it. Instead, container gardeners devoted to organic methodology turn to potting mixtures that contain 50% highly fluffy components and 50% nutrient-dense compost.

For the fluff factor, you can use sphagnum moss, coconut coir, vermiculite, perlite, or (better yet) a mixture of each, adding limestone as necessary to mitigate acidic pH. On the other hand, if you don't want to purchase potting soils containing these amendments, I recommend the stump dirt that I write about in detail in chapter 17.

Fluff factors act to prevent compaction (a big problem in pots) while also holding onto moisture that would otherwise quickly bake out of small volumes of soil. But there's very little nutrition for your plants to find in the potting-soil components listed above. That's why container gardeners fill the other half of each pot with a high-quality compost, while also including smaller amounts of organic fertilizers like blood meal, soft rock phosphate, greensand, and Azomite. Finally, potted vegetables are usually fed a liquid fertilizer such as compost tea as often as once a month during the growing season to ensure nutrient levels stay high in the small root space.

Another difference between container and in-ground gardening comes in the fall. While the earth in your vegetable garden will likely become richer every year, most container gardeners toss out their used potting soil each season. Don't just throw that used soil in the trash, though. Instead, old potting soil makes a good soil-amendment to be top-dressed onto in-ground garden beds. There won't be many nutrients left behind, but the organic matter will be appreciated by your non-potted ecosystem. On the other hand, one of our blog readers has had good results reusing Pro-Mix brand soil, which she amends with a generous helping of compost and granular organic fertilizer at the beginning of each growing season before putting the revamped potting soil back into her containers.

Photo credit: Kiina Tobey

Kiina uses pallets to lift her containers up out of the shade of nearby raised beds. Sliding pots around throughout the day also helps to optimize sun in her partially shady conditions.

If this description of growing vegetables in pots sounds like a lot more muss and fuss that simply planting seeds in the ground . . . it is. But there are several very valid reasons to prefer containers over in-earth growing. Kiina in Virginia explained, "I use containers as a way to add more space to the garden without adding more raised beds and taking away too much 'lawn.' Containers also let me squeeze things a little closer together than normal plant spacing guidelines suggest. It's in a pot, their roots won't compete, so plants in pots can be shoved closer together, which helps in a smaller space."

Meanwhile, Heather grows her food in zone 3 in Canada where the nights are cold and the days are sunny and dry. She notes, "I find things grow much better in pots than in my raised beds." In particular, heat-lovers like peppers and Mediterranean herbs may prefer pot culture even if you don't live in the frigid north. Growing in containers also allows you to bring vegetables inside for a few extra weeks of production when freezes threaten summer vegetables at the end of the growing season.

If you'd like to learn more about growing edibles in pots, I recommend *The Vegetable Gardener's Container Bible* by Edward C. Smith. The author includes step-by-step instructions for building DIY self-watering planters, which are bound to make your container experiments easier and more successful. Smith also walks you through choosing vegetables, mixing soil, and otherwise managing edibles in pots. Just remember—container earth is nothing like in-ground soil, so you'll need to learn the ropes all over again if you want to grow vegetables in pots.

Aquaponics

Aquaponics allows you to raise both fish and plants in the same space. This setup is found in the greenhouse of Virginia Highlands Community College in Abingdon, Virginia.

Or maybe you don't need soil at all. Aquaponics combines aquaculture and hydroponics, feeding plants with fish waste then returning clean, aerated water to the tank so your finned friends don't choke. There are worms and bacteria involved too, with these smaller critters converting ammonia from the fish poop into nitrites and nitrates that plants can consume while also cleaning up decaying roots and larger particles of fish waste. In other words, aquaponics promises to create a closed loop that produces two crops, each relying on the waste product of the other in order to thrive.

Unfortunately, despite the inherent elegance of this human-created ecosystem, I don't recommend aquaponics for most home gardeners. First of all, there's the issue of electricity. You'll need pumps and heaters and (often) grow lights since aquaponics systems do best indoors unless you live in a tropical climate. Then there's the vast quantities of fish food you have to bring in from outside the system, proving that aquaponics isn't actually a closed loop.

In the end, I feel like aquaponics only makes sense in areas like the one in which it originated—urban Australia. There, moderate winter temperatures allow many homesteaders to keep their aquaponic setups outdoors year-round. Meanwhile, rain in Australia is so scarce that minimizing water use may trump minimizing electricity consumption, especially in cities where good soil is scarce.

That said, it's quite possible that I'm down on aquaponics simply because I adore dirt and there's no soil involved. And I can also see how aquaponics would make sense in a home-scale greenhouse since the fishes' water would provide thermal mass, buffering daytime high temperatures and nighttime lows. Meanwhile, I've read about at least one temperate-climate homesteader who uses a year-round, outdoor water garden to run a summer-only aquaponic setup growing lettuce and other short-lived plants.

So you might be able to put on your thinking cap and make a lower-energy version of aquaponics work for you. If that sounds intriguing, I recommend checking out Sylvia Bernstein's *Aquaponic Gardening* to get you started. The book walks readers through setting up various types of aquaponic systems and will definitely help you—and your fish, and your plants, and your worms—get on the right track in no time.

PART 3

BALANCING NUTRIENTS AND ACIDITY

Remineralization adds nutrients back into your soil to ensure a bountiful, delicious harvest.

In *The Intelligent Gardener*, Steve Solomon makes a solid case for balancing soil nutrients in a process known as remineralization. He based his recommendations on others' research, but also on his own experiences with discovering that home-grown food doesn't always lead to good health.

Solomon's first-person account will likely resonate with other homesteaders. He and his wife lived for nine years in Oregon, where they grew most of their own food on worn-out soil that was deficient in several major nutrients. As a result, the couple began experiencing lowered energy levels, loose teeth, and soft fingernails.

A six-month vacation in Fiji created dramatic changes in the Solomons' vitality, due (the husband believed) to the local produce grown in soil fertilized by silt from volcanic rocks. This experience led him to the work of Weston Price, who argued that we really need four (or more) times the recommended daily allowance of calcium, magnesium, phosphorus, iron, and vitamins A, D, and E for optimal health. Next, Solomon turned to the work of remineralization guru William Albrecht, who explained that if we want to consume those high levels of vitamins and minerals, gardeners must plant into well-balanced soil chock full of minerals.

While Solomon's tale is intriguing, many organic gardeners are rightfully leery of the similarities between remineralization and mainstream, non-organic farming since both utilize chemical fertilizers. In the latter scenario, nitrogen, phosphorus and potassium are applied in their most basic form before each crop, creating a cycle of dependency in the soil. For example, if a farmer pours on chemical nitrogen fertilizers, the nitrogen-cycling microorganisms in his soil perish, and the farmer is forced to continue applying chemical nitrogen fertilizers if he wants subsequent crops to grow. The result is impoverished soil that decreases in quality every year.

For that reason, most readers of this book will choose compost over chemicals for annual fertilization. So why would you apply deficient minerals in chemical form if remineralization is likely to produce the same decline in soil microorganisms that you'd see from traditional chemical farming? Proponents of the former method will rebut that remineralization is meant to be a one-time corrective action to combat the natural effects of leaching, so you can consider the fertilizer applications in this scenario as a bit like tilling up the ground before building permanent raised beds—a necessary short-term evil to produce long-term gains.

Many proponents of remineralization use a Brix meter to assess the nutrient density of their crops. However, you should be aware that Brix is simply a measurement of sugar content and you can get the same information with your own taste buds.

In the end, remineralization is one of the most controversial topics covered in this book, and I'll admit that I'm not entirely sold on the concept myself. But it's worth understanding the whys and hows of this slightly fringe technique in order to decide which, if any, facets of remineralization you want to utilize in your own garden.

Chapter 11:
Correcting Soil pH

When and Why to Shift pH

Blueberries require a much more acidic soil than other common edibles.

Even though this chapter is included under the remineralization umbrella, tweaking pH to suit your garden plants uses much more mainstream science than other parts of a remineralization campaign. In fact, most gardeners have a need to correct pH at some point in their growing careers and the task is generally accomplished in roughly the same manner. So why do I put pH under the remineralization umbrella? Because pH management utilizes the same science as topping up other garden paucities, which lends credence to the remineralization hypothesis and also helps you understand how to decide on the proper amendments to correct other common soil deficits.

In contrast to other types of remineralization, though, the need to shift soil pH is so common and widespread that many gardeners work to sweeten their soil as a matter of course, spreading lime or wood ashes on gardens and fields annually without first testing to determine whether the application is needed. And, if you treat your garden with regular doses of chemical fertilizers, you may need that preemptive liming since most chemical fertilizers tend to acidify the ground. However, if you're an organic gardener, it's much safer to determine whether and how much your pH is out of whack using a soil test before embarking on a liming campaign.

Even though I strongly recommend soil tests before tweaking pH, I should mention that you *can* make some educated guesses about your soil's tendency to change pH over time based on your region and climate. For example, young soils tend to be acidic if they lie atop granite, sandstone, or shale, while soils that began life as limestone are more likely to be alkaline.

Regardless of the bedrock, though, a soil's initial pH will inevitably change over time depending on your area's average rainfall. Just as leaching carries away nutrients in wet soil, the same heavy rains also tend to acidify the ground in high-rainfall climates. On the other hand, water slowly moves up into the topsoil from deep underground in regions where rainfall is scarce, and that subirrigated liquid carries along sodium and calcium, increasing the soil's alkalinity in the process.

But please consider that I've offered the preceding information solely to help you understand the bigger picture. I stick firmly to my recommendation that you *must* perform a soil test before you mess around with pH (or with any other type of remineralization for that matter). Then, if your soil's pH tests lower than 6 or greater than 7, it's probably worth at least considering neutralizing amendments. Your goal in this case is to achieve a pH around 6.5, which will maximize nutrient availability for most vegetables. Or, if you're growing blueberries—the one common edible that requires a very different level of acidity—you should aim for a pH of 4.5 to 5.5 for northern highbush or for 6 or lower for rabbiteye blueberries.

You can get an idea of what your garden soil looked like before you began improving it by testing unimproved ground nearby. Our chicken pastures show that our garden started out as acidic, nutrient-poor dirt.

The rest of this chapter will explain chemical methods of changing soil pH using lime and sulfur. However, I'd remiss if I didn't mention that quick fixes in this department, just as in other soil-improvement campaigns, will harm your micro-organisms in the short term and will require regular reapplications as your soil begins to veer back toward its natural pH. The slower but surer approach is to add lots of quality organic matter since humus has a buffering effect on pH and tends to sweeten acidic soil while lowering the pH of soil with excessive alkalinity.

For example, even though I didn't perform a soil test before bringing my current garden into line, I can take a snapshot backwards in time by considering the earth found in nearby pastures. These areas haven't enjoyed any soil renovation at all, short of plenty of nitrogen deposited in the form of chicken manure from the birds that graze there. And those unimproved pastures prove the point that a wet climate leads to acidic soil, since the pH of each pasture clocks in between 5 and 6.

In stark contrast, the garden areas just a few feet away that have been treated to years of compost, mulch, hugelkultur, and cover cropping showcase a much more palatable pH that ranges from 6.9 to 7.3. In other words, adding organic matter has taken my overly acidic soil and made it almost *too* alkaline, all without applying an ounce of lime. Good thing I didn't follow my neighbors' recommendations to spread powdered limestone on my garden every year as a matter of course.

Chemistry of pH

Heavy rains cause leaching by washing nutrients out of the soil.

My garden story aside, you can probably guess that changing pH with organic matter takes time. And if you decide to try out the faster, chemical approach to pH management instead, you'll need to understand a bit of chemistry.

Remember CEC—cation exchange capacity—that I mentioned in chapter 5? This concept is key to understanding both pH management and remineralization, so I'm going to bore you with a bit of in-depth chemistry here. Feel free to skip ahead to the next section if your eyes glaze over and you just want actionable information.

Still here? Okay, you may recall that CEC levels are higher in soils that are rich in organic matter and clay. But what does that really mean?

If you ever took a chemistry class, you'll probably recall that cations are positively charged particles. In your soil, several of the most important plant nutrients turn out to be cations, including calcium, magnesium, and potassium. The trouble is that these cations will happily float along in the water between your soil particles, which means they quickly wash away during heavy rains if the nutrients don't have anything to grab hold of during the deluge. (This is the chemical explanation for leaching.)

Luckily, in chemistry as in human life, opposites attract. And two components of your soil—organic matter and clay— contain plenty of surface area with a negative charge, so these particles act like magnets pulling cations toward them. Just as iron filings attached to a magnet don't fall to the ground when you tilt the sheet of paper they're lying upon, soil nutrients stuck onto clay or organic matter don't leach away when water washes through your garden dirt. Instead, the positively charged nutrients end up hanging out just where your plant roots want them, ensuring that your crops have plenty of access to the calcium, magnesium, and potassium that they need in order to grow and thrive.

Which brings us to the cation exchange capacity of your soil, which you can think of as a measurement of how many of these positively charged nutrients are able to bind onto soil particles rather than floating around in the liquidy soup in between. In other words, CEC measures the size of the container you can pour cations into before they overflow out the top. If your soil suffers from a low CEC, then excess nutrients added to the garden are just going to wash away during the next heavy rain. In contrast, a high CEC means you've got lots of space for adding calcium, magnesium, and potassium to your garden and expecting these nutrients to stay put.

A high cation exchange capacity equates to a healthy, resilient garden ecosystem.

Here's where it gets a bit more complicated—not all cations are created equal. Instead, certain types of nutrients bind tighter to your soil particles than others, and the amount of each nutrient type present will also impact who gets a spot on those important cation-exchange sites.

Imagine for a moment that your soil is hosting a game of musical chairs played between surly, burly muscle-builders and puny, meek kindergartners. If there are ten chairs in the room, ten bodybuilders, and ten kindergarteners, I'll bet you can guess who's going to end up in the chairs when the music stops—all ten bodybuilders. On the other hand, if there are ten chairs, a hundred kindergarteners, and only one body-builder, that big guy might not find a spot to sit when surrounded by the patter of so many tiny feet.

Getting back to the world of soil, you can think of calcium as the burly bodybuilder and hydrogen as the petite kindergartener. Magnesium, potassium, and sodium follow a line of descending bond strength, fitting between those two extremes. So if you dump masses of lime (which is mostly calcium) into your soil, those strong calcium ions will fill all of the cation-exchange spots, bumping off most of the weaker cations. Meanwhile, if you only add a moderate amount of calcium, only the lowest cations on the totem pole will be bumped off, so you'll end up with a higher ratio of calcium and a lower ratio of sodium and hydrogen in the soil.

But what does this have to do with pH? I didn't bore you with the relevant chemistry before, but now you need to understand that the pH scale is really a measurement of how many hydrogen ions are present in a given substance. And, counterintuitively, a lower pH means that there are *more* hydrogen ions available. So you can think of an acidic soil as having too many hydrogen ions floating around making trouble. In fact, when it comes to soil, if hydrogen has to fill *any* of your cation-exchange sites, that means your dirt is on the acidic side of the pH scale.

Now, you may recall that the lowest cation on the totem pole is hydrogen, which is pulled out of water to fill empty spots only if there aren't enough other cations to go around. Which is why adding lime to your soil raises the pH. The extra calcium in lime knocks hydrogen ions off your soil particles and back to their regular job of floating around in the water. There, hydrogen ions can merge with the carbonate supplied by the lime, creating additional water and carbon dioxide.

Both water and carbon dioxide move easily out of soil, so the excess hydrogen is washed away after your application of lime, resulting in soil that is no longer acidic. In our metaphorical game of musical chairs, the kindergarteners have been sent back to school, so only the bodybuilders are left to fight over those chairs.

Phew! I know that was a long description that you don't really need to know just to tweak your soil's pH levels. But hopefully it'll give you a head start on understanding the intricacies of remineralization that I'll present in the next chapter. Plus, I always find it useful to know what I'm doing when I add an amendment to the earth. Regardless of whether you read or skimmed, though, it's finally time for some hands-on information about how to bringing unruly pH into balance.

Dealing with Acidic Soil

Be sure to check your bag of lime to see whether you've bought agricultural lime (which simply supplies calcium) or dolomitic lime (which supplies both calcium and magnesium).

Whether or not you understand the chemistry of pH management, changing the pH of acidic soil is as simple as applying a certain amount of lime to your garden, then sitting back to wait for the amendment to get to work. That said, I don't recommend that the home gardener do the math for application rates herself since elements like CEC have to be factored into the analysis. Instead, you should take a look at your soil-test report, which will almost certainly suggest a certain number of pounds or tons per acre if your pH is out of whack.

Given that information, your math becomes simple. If the recommended lime-application rate is provided in tons per acre, simply divide the number by 22 to find out how many pounds you should apply per square foot in your garden. In contrast, if the recommended lime dosage is in pounds per acre, divide by 43,560 to find pounds per square feet.

Assuming you know how much lime to apply, the next question is—where does that lime come from? Farm-supply stores will likely offer several different products, and it's easy to become confused when faced with a sea of liming options. First of all, I recommend narrowing down your choices based on what kind of lime is in the bag. Agricultural lime (sometimes called aglime, lime, ground limestone, or calcitic limestone) is the standard and is the safest option if you don't know anything else about your soil. Dolomite (also known as dolomitic limestone) contains magnesium as well as calcium, which is handy if you're deficient in that second nutrient, but which can cause problems if your soil suffers from an overabundance of magnesium. In the latter scenario, be sure to read the lime bag carefully since some products don't mention which type of mineral is contained inside. Dolomitic limestone will always mention magnesium even if the word "dolomite" is absent from the amendment's packaging.

In the case of either agricultural lime or dolomitic lime, you'll usually also be given a choice between different particle sizes. Pulverized lime is the finest ground dust, which means the amendment acts relatively quickly but also tends to blow around in the wind and to clog machinery. If you're spreading lime by hand, though, and are careful not to breath in the powder, pulverized lime is a good choice for the home garden. The other options are pelletized or granular lime, both of which will act a little slower but won't have the dust problems you'll find with pulverized lime.

Blossom-end rot in tomatoes is a classic sign of calcium deficiency. However, the deeper source of this disorder isn't usually insufficient calcium in the soil. Instead, drought, root damage, excessive heat, or rapid plant growth can all make it tough for a tomato plant to take up enough calcium to form perfect fruits. So seeing a darkened spot on the bottom of your tomatoes isn't a good enough reason to apply lime to the soil. Instead, mulch well and water regularly, then blossom-end rot will soon be a thing of the past.

Beyond agricultural and dolomitic limestone, there are three other liming options to consider. Quick lime and burnt lime are faster acting than traditional ground limestone, but both are harder to handle and are more likely to get your pH out of whack. If you're not an expert, I recommend skipping these amendments.

Wood ashes are a more traditional homestead liming agent since many farmers heat with wood and have ashes on hand as a waste product. I write more about ashes in chapter 18, but for now let me simply warn you away from using this amendment to impact your soil's pH. As the first strike against ashes, the fluffy powder is very high in potassium, which is problematic if your soil is already overloaded with that nutrient. More troublesome for those of you who might appreciate a potassium pick-me-up, the pH-mitigation effects of wood ashes are much more variable than the effects of packaged limestone. So if you want to use ashes, I recommend applying much less than you think you need, then performing another soil test a year later to see what effects your ash application had on the garden plot.

Okay, let's assume you know what kind of lime you're going to apply and how much your garden needs. How do you get the lime into the soil? First, pick the appropriate time of year. Lime requires at least two or three fallow months in order to react with the hydrogen in your soil, so you're better off liming in the fall or early winter to prepare for a spring planting. And be sure to water the lime into the ground if your off season is dry since the amendment won't start acting until the particles are fully wet.

The other important decision pertaining to lime application is whether to top-dress (scatter the amendment across the surface of the ground) or to mix the amendment into the topsoil. If you've got an option—for example, if you're building a new raised bed and will be churning up the soil anyway—lime will act much more quickly if it's mixed into the earth. On the other hand, no-till gardeners *can* get some of the same effects by simply top-dressing onto an unbroken soil surface, especially if they apply mulch on top of the lime. In healthy gardens, earthworms have been shown to transport surface-applied lime down at least seven inches into the earth, so your pH mitigation effects will likely work their way into no-till ground slowly but surely.

Dealing with Alkaline Soil

Yellowing between the veins on blueberry leaves is a classic sign of iron deficiency caused by high pH.

While bringing acidic soil back into line with lime is a common agricultural technique, many gardeners choose to simply live with overly alkaline ground. The trouble is that lowering pH is much more expensive than raising it, and the common acidifying amendment—sulfur—takes even longer to work than lime does. As a result, most soil scientists only recommend applying sulfur to your garden if you're planting a very acid-loving crop like blueberries or if you want to help a small patch of ornamentals like azaleas thrive.

In terms of actual application rates, I'll once again send you to your test reports since soil buffering capacity complicates what would otherwise be a straightforward equation. However, just as with lime, there are options to consider when it comes to which amendment you select. The most common option is elemental sulfur, which is also the cheapest acidifying amendment. However, elemental sulfur requires the actions of microorganisms before the amendment can impact your pH, meaning that elemental sulfur must be applied during the spring or summer prior to next year's planting rather than the winter before. Iron sulfate works faster, but you need about six times as much of this amendment compared to elemental sulfur. Finally, aluminum sulfate is only recommended for use with hydrangeas since the metallic half of the compound can cause toxic responses in other types of plants.

No matter which type of sulfur you choose to apply, the rules for actually getting the amendment into your ground are very similar to those pertaining to lime. Small particles (powders) act fastest, as do amendments actually mixed into the earth rather than spread on top. But since you're probably planting perennials that won't appreciate having their roots messed with later, you might consider including some larger particle sizes than are recommended during liming since big chunks of sulfur will act as time-delayed acidifiers, keeping the soil sour for several years into the future.

If you're like me, you're probably wondering if there's a more organic approach to acidifying garden ground. Peat moss is the option most often discussed by soil scientists, but various gardeners on the Internet also suggest incorporating tea bags, citrus peels, or pine needles into your soil to lower the pH enough for blueberries to grow. In my own garden, I

The blueberry bush in the foreground was planted into soil amended with sulfur while the bush in the background was planted into soil amended with pine needles.

decided to test the effects of using leaf mold scraped up from beneath pine trees then mixed into the earth as I planted new blueberry bushes. To that end, half of my blueberry plants received a few gallons of pine mold while the other half were treated to elemental sulfur mixed into their soil. And as much as I hate to admit it, the chemical approach was much more effective, with the classic signs of iron deficiency (a reaction to high pH) showing up in the blueberries treated with only rotten pine needles while the sulfur-treated plants thrived.

However, there *is* hope for organic acidification. After several years of top-dressing my blueberry patch with composted manure, sidedressing with rotting pine logs, and mulching with pine needles, straw, and leaves, all signs of iron deficiency disappeared from both sets of blueberry plants. And when you understand why blueberries flounder in alkaline soil, these results make sense. High pH is only a problem for blueberries because required nutrients like iron aren't as readily available at a pH above 5 or 6. But adding lots of organic matter to soil increases the availability of all nutrients, counteracting that perceived deficiency. Meanwhile, microorganisms hard at work decomposing organic matter tend to create acidic pockets even within alkaline soil. So it's possible that you can get by with planting blueberries in neutral ground without adding sulfur . . . but only if you're willing to embark on a campaign of topping up your organic-matter levels annually and dealing with a few signs of deficiency during the plants' early years.

Chapter 12:
Remineralization Basics

Do I Need to Remineralize?

Remineralization replaces nutrients leached away by rain.

As with pH, whether or not your garden could benefit from remineralization is largely dependent upon your area's rocks and rain. You may recall that the type of bedrock dissolving to create the soil in your garden is responsible for determining which minerals were there in the first place. Some rocks, like those in Fiji, are more well-rounded than others. But even if your bedrock is perfect, excessive rainfall can still wash those nutrients out of the earth through a process known as leaching.

You can get a rough idea of your garden's leaching potential by considering where you live. Hot, dry areas like the American Southwest suffer from little or no leaching because all of the water that hits the ground is sucked up by plants or simply evaporates from the earth's surface. At the other extreme, New England soils are strongly affected by leaching because cold weather keeps precipitation in the ground once it hits. As a result, water tends to gush through the topsoil and into the groundwater in these temperate, wet climates, carrying more minerals away with each rain or bout of melting snow.

In general, most of the soils in the eastern United States have been depleted by leaching unless careful stewardship has kept organic matter levels high at all times. Remember how humus holds onto the same minerals that rain tries to remove? This fact gives us a clue about how to counteract leaching. By boosting organic matter levels, we keep nutrients cycling even if our soils are overwhelmed with frequent and heavy rains.

Another factor to consider is the age of your dirt. Young soils have lots of minerals, but over time, rocks in the earth completely dissolve and stop adding nutrients into the ground. In addition, the cation exchange capacities of soils tend to degrade over geologic time if we don't increase organic-matter levels, so older soils have a lessened ability to hold onto any nutrients that do show up. Here's where the southeast is even worse off than New England—we haven't had glaciers down here recently to top off our rock reserves, so many soils are particularly old and low on minerals.

The organic gardener in the crowd is surely yelling at me by now. "Why not just fix any potential imbalances with compost?" she asks. "After all, enough compost will repair just about any soil woe." Unfortunately, if you're trying to refresh your minerals using compost created from local manure and vegetation, your amendments will suffer from the same deficiencies that were present in your soil in the first place. For example, low calcium in the soil will result in calcium-deficient plants, and those calcium-deficient plants will produce calcium-deficient compost. Short of trucking in organic matter from a distant source, the solution appears to be taking a soil test to determine exactly which nutrients your soil is low on, then correcting those imbalances with a focused remineralization campaign.

On the other hand, the devil's advocate position states that remineralization isn't as scientific as it sounds. Even core practitioners will tell you that there have been no side-by-side experiments in which one plot of land was remineralized while a control plot was left alone, with harvests from each plot being carefully measured. So whether remineralization actually makes a difference in the average garden is up for debate.

In addition, you should be aware that there are also serious downsides to the process, such as cost and mineral burn. So I'm requesting that you read this chapter critically, analyze what I say with your thinking cap turned up to high, and then make your own decision about whether remineralization is right for you.

Goals of Remineralization

If you do decide to take the leap, there are several different ways to go about remineralizing. The official method focuses on balancing the ratios of a few important nutrients in your soil, topping up those you're low on at the same time you flush excessive amounts of others out of your ground. For example, the most well-known remineralization advocate, William Albrecht, was primarily interested in calcium, magnesium, potassium, and sodium, the proportions of which he suggested should match the ratio found in prairie soils—68:12:4:2. Other practitioners have suggested slightly different ratios, such as 62:18:4:2 for sandy soil, or 85:5:3:1.5 if you're following the work of Victor Tiedjens and think calcium is of utmost importance.

If you're interested in this type of ratio-based remineralization, I highly recommend finding a copy of Steve Solomon's *The Intelligent Gardener* and using his worksheets to delve into the intricacies of remineralization formulas. I won't repeat that information here because the calculations are too in-depth for this book.

On the other hand, another way of looking at remineralization is to use amendments to correct specific issues that you've already identified in your soil. For example, Solomon writes that excessive potassium is a common problem in organic gardens grown in leached ground, especially if you regularly add hay, straw, or wood products to your garden in the form of compost or mulch. High potassium levels have the benefit of making plants grow quickly, but the resulting produce tends to be low in protein, high in carbohydrates, and deficient in calcium and phosphorus. Solomon posits that livestock eating plants grown on high-potassium soil gain weight but don't breed well, and people who dine on the products of that type of soil tend to put on the pounds and have health problems as well. So if your soil test comes back with potassium levels considerably higher than the recommended value, it can be worth using lime (if you want to sweeten the soil too) or gypsum (if your pH is okay) to flush excessive potassium out of your garden.

Theoretically, gypsum can be used to loosen soil and relieve waterlogging problems. In practice, if your groundwater is very high, gypsum won't have much of an effect.

Another soil issue that might be resolved by a focused remineralization campaign is problematic texture. For example, clay-rich soil that's also high in magnesium tends to be very tight and waterlogged. Adding lots of calcium to this type of soil (often in the form of gypsum if you don't want to impact pH) can flush excess magnesium away while fluffing up problematic ground in the process.

I have to admit that adding gypsum to my high-magnesium, waterlogged soil made little difference, presumably because the underlying problem in my case was actually a wet climate and an elevated water table. Still, if you'd like to try gypsum on your own wet ground, it's relatively safe to do so even without performing a soil test. Recommended application rates vary widely, but run as high as 2,000 pounds per acre (equivalent to a pound for every 22 square feet).

On another note, those of you gardening near the coast and irrigating with water high in salts may be suffering from excessive sodium in your soil. This cation tightens up soil even more so than magnesium does. And, as an added game changer, sodium can also be toxic to plants in even moderate amounts. Luckily, salt is pretty easy to flush out of soil by applying extra calcium in the form of lime or gypsum since only hydrogen is lower on the cation totem pole than sodium is.

A final valid reason to consider remineralization is to boost levels of essential plant micronutrients that might be missing from your soil. While chasing the perfect ratio of calcium to magnesium to potassium to sodium may or may not make any difference in your garden, a micronutrient deficiency can often be tasted in your crops and can indeed carry over to create a deficiency in your diet.

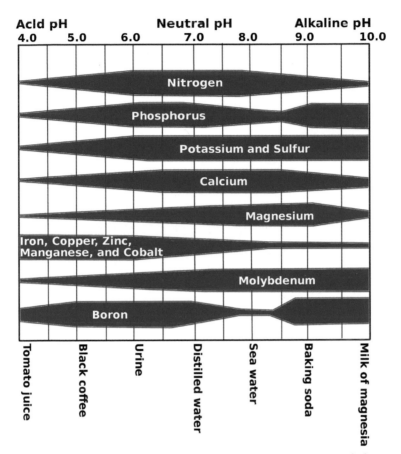

A perceived micronutrient deficiency could be due to improper pH. For example, boron becomes dramatically less available to plants above a pH of 7.

If you're serious about monitoring micronutrients, you might consider a plant-tissue test to round out your soil-testing results since the former are more effective at capturing micronutrient problems and will help you pinpoint deficiencies that may be the root of your vegetables' failure to thrive. But keep in mind that micronutrient problems can also be very pH dependent since most micronutrients are dramatically less available at non-garden-friendly pHs. Perhaps you really just need to deal with an acidity or alkalinity problem after all?

Choosing Amendments for Remineralization

Micronutrients can be found in their chemical form or in weaker amendments such as kelp, seaweed, and rock powders.

Before I delve deeper into remineralization amendments, it's important to understand the distinction between macronutrients and micronutrients. In terms of the former, plants require so much of three macronutrients—nitrogen, phosphorus, and potassium—that most farmers try to add these nutrients to the field before every crop as a matter of course. In fact, agricultural amendments are often labeled with an NPK value to make the math easier for farmers. This three-number sequence lists the percent by weight of nitrogen, phosphorus, and potassium (in that order), and the table on the next page lists the NPK values of a few common organic fertilizers.

NPK values of common organic fertilizers

Fertilizer	NPK	Notes
Bat guano	10 : 3 : 1 or 3 : 10 : 1	Processing method will determine fertilizer profile
Blood meal	12 : 1 : 1	Can burn plants due to high nitrogen levels
Fish meal	10 : 6 : 0	
Alfalfa meal	2 : 1: 2	
Corn gluten meal	9 : 0 : 0	Inhibits seed germination, so can be used for weed control around existing plants; usually GMO
Cottonseed meal	6 : 4 : 1.5	High in pesticide residues; usually GMO
Soybean meal	7 : 2 : 1	Usually GMO
Raw bone meal	3 : 22 : 0	Phosphorus from bone meal is only available in soils with a pH below 7
Steamed bone meal	1 : 15 : 0	Phosphorus from bone meal is only available in soils with a pH below 7
Granite dust	0 : 0 : 4	Includes trace minerals as well as potassium
Greensand	0 : 0 : 3	Includes trace minerals as well as potassium
Wood ashes	0 : 1 : 4	

What you should be aware of is that these three macronutrients usually aren't included in a remineralization analysis except in the case of a potential excess of potassium. Instead, I'll assume that you're adding sufficient quantities of nitrogen, phosphorus, and potassium in your regular compost applications, possibly boosted by the purchased fertilizers listed above.

Next, calcium, magnesium, and sulfur are also considered macronutrients since these three elements are used in relatively large quantities by plants. However, soils are much less likely to be deficient in these three nutrients, so you'll usually only need to add so-called secondary macronutrients to your soil if you're seeking to create optimal ratios recommended by remineralization advocates. I've mentioned some mainstream sources of these three nutrients previously, but I'll give you a more comprehensive list here. Calcium is often added to the soil in the form of lime or gypsum, but can also be found in large quantities in bone meal, oyster shells, Montana hard rock phosphate, and calphos. Magnesium is most often applied as dolomitic limestone, and sulfur is found in gypsum or in agricultural sulfur.

In contrast to the six macronutrients mentioned above, micronutrients are used by plants in very small quantities, but they are no less essential for optimal plant growth. Depending on who you talk to, there are anywhere between six and thirteen micronutrients. If you go for the larger picture, the elements that are required by plants in small quantities include: boron, chlorine, cobalt, copper, fluorine, iodine, iron, manganese, molybdenum, selenium, silicon, sodium, and zinc. Of these, many soil tests only report boron, copper, and zinc . . . or perhaps none at all. So it can be hard to get a handle on whether your soil has any deficiencies in the micronutrient department.

Unfortunately, when it comes to applying micronutrients to your garden soil, the waters are similarly murky. First, you'll need to decide between strong chemical fertilizers and mild biological sources. In the latter category, rock powders (sometimes known as granite dust or rock dust) are a common choice to add a variety of micronutrients back into the soil since the dusts don't cause problems by burning plant roots, building up unwanted salts, changing the pH, and shocking microbes. On the other hand, the efficacy of these powders is questionable since the pulverized stones have to be further broken down in your soil before they release any of the minerals you're missing. Best-case scenario, rock powders are very slow acting; worst-case scenario, they don't actually do any good. If you're planning on investing in rock powders, it's probably best to splurge on Azomite, a proprietary name for a rock powder that began life as volcanic ash combined with seawater. The minerals in the seawater component, at least, will be immediately available to your plants.

More effective than rock powders but also much more expensive are biological amendments that began life in the ocean. Remember how leaching carries nutrients out of your soil in a great gush of water? All of those leached minerals eventually end up in the seven seas, so it seems like poetic justice to bring ocean products back to land in order to remineralize your garden. To this end, kelp and seaweed can both be purchased in powdered form to be spread on the garden (or fed to animals). Sea salt also contains a host of micronutrients, but the sodium levels are too high for large applications unless your soil is also deficient in that salt. Alternatively, if you live near the shore, you can simply harvest seaweed that has washed up on beaches after a storm.

The trouble with rock powders, kelp, and seaweed is that you can't use them to supply one particular micronutrient rather than topping up the soil's stores of each element. So if you want to follow remineralization guidelines and bring all of your nutrients into balance, you'll instead turn to chemical fertilizers. Sulfate salts are the cheapest and fastest-acting alternative in this regard, but more biologically benign alternatives exist if you're willing to pay for the privilege of protecting your microbes. Chelates mimic the way micronutrients are bound to humus in the soil and fritted trace elements (a.k.a. FTEs or frits) are another slow-release option for micronutrient remineralization.

Finally, foliar feeding (spraying liquid fertilizers directly onto plant leaves) isn't part of a long-term remineralization campaign, but the method is often advocated by soil scientists as the best way to correct micronutrient deficiencies in plants. In particular, foliar feeding is a good option if plant-tissue tests show that your crops are deficient in calcium and other nutrients that don't move easily between plant cells.

Seed Meals

Nitrogen can be in short supply when direct-seeding into cold soil.

Before I go on, this seems like a good spot to address seed meals, which are used by some organic gardeners as fertilizers but are applied in much the same manner as remineralization amendments. The benefit of these high-nitrogen meals is that they're much lighter weight and easier to handle than traditional, organic sources of nitrogen such as compost and manure. On the other hand, seed meals don't provide the same heaping helping of organic matter to the garden, so I eschew their use on my own plot.

Despite my own reluctance to water down the Kool-Aid with seed meals, Steve Solomon makes a strong case for the necessity of highly accessible forms of nitrogen in cold spring gardens in his book *Gardening When It Counts*. Solomon notes that the bacteria responsible for decomposing organic matter to produce plant-friendly nitrogen are sound asleep when the weather is frigid, which leads to slow plant growth in very early spring. So stronger doses of nitrogen are necessary at that time to counteract the drowsy winter microbes.

But while Solomon's biological analysis makes sense, I've had no problem with low nitrogen levels despite pushing the early-spring-gardening envelope to the limit, planting peas and lettuce into soil with temperatures barely above freezing. Why the lack of nitrogen deficiency with my cool-weather crops? I encourage fungi and actinomycetes with no-till gardening practices (see chapter 13) throughout the year, which means that these microorganisms are ready and willing to break down organic matter even in extremely cold weather in my garden plot. So even if you're farming in Alaska, choosing the right techniques might obviate the necessity of seed meals.

Despite this rebuttal, I can understand how the backbreaking work of spreading manure and compost can get old for some. So if you're determined to try out seed meals, you'll want to be aware of a few specifics about their use. First of all, these meals are applied annually to your garden before planting crops just like compost would be, but you may need to increase your lime quota since cottonseed meal, particularly, has a tendency to acidify ground. Corn gluten meal has another unique quality—the amendment inhibits seedling germination. This characteristic can be a bonus if you apply corn gluten meal to the soil surface after your crop plants are already up and running or when transplanting already thriving seedlings, but you won't want to spread corn gluten meal along a row of newly planted vegetable seeds the way you might apply another organic fertilizer.

You should also be aware that seed meals are agricultural byproducts that usually come from crops genetically modified to produce *Bacillus thuringiensis* (Bt). While I don't knee-jerk against GMO products, I personally eschew the use of Bt even though the chemical is considered an organic-approved pesticide. The trouble is that Bt kills a wide range of insects (including beneficials), and Bt has also been shown to be toxic to people and the environment in at least some studies. I don't like to think of Bt being carried along into my garden in seed meals, so I consider that another strike against this gardening shortcut.

What are other lightweight, high-nitrogen alternatives to seed meals? If you can afford the expense, guano, blood meal, and fish meal are all animal products that act much like seed meals in the garden. On the other hand, penny-pinchers will find that homegrown chicken manure is similarly high in nitrogen, while human urine can be watered down to provide fast nitrogen for garden plants. And of course, there are always the more traditional composts and manures, which I write about in much more depth in part four of this book. Because it really *is* worth a bit of heavy shoveling to add organic matter to your soil along with nitrogen if you want to ensure the long-term health of your garden plot.

How to Remineralize Your Soil

Once you figure out exactly why and what you want to apply to your soil, the actual act of remineralization is very similar to applying lime to sweeten your pH. In fact, if you have any intention of liming your ground, it's best to do so first and give the amendment time to work before going back in to balance macronutrients and top up micronutrients several months later. Remember, adding those bullying calcium cations can push everyone else off the musical chairs that make up your cation exchange capacity. So you're throwing money away if you add other amendments one year then lime the next rather than vice versa.

Remineralization is best performed in the winter since many of the amendments can burn growing plants.

Assuming you aren't going to lime or that you've already limed in a previous season, now's the time to use Solomon's worksheets to determine exactly how much of each remineralization amendment you want to add to your soil. I recommend mixing amendments that you'll use in small quantities first, then applying bulkier amendments like gypsum separately. Otherwise, the fine powders tend to filter down to the bottom of your wheelbarrow, meaning you apply too much in one spot and too little in the next. (Yes, I *am* writing from personal experience. Thanks for asking. My goal is to make all of the stupid mistakes right up front so you don't have to repeat them.)

These strawberry plants were burned by my application of micronutrient salts even though I waited until the dormant season to remineralize.

Your goal should be to apply amendments while plants are dormant, but this may not be entirely possible in a four-season garden. When I remineralized, I went ahead and scattered gypsum and micronutrient salts across the entire garden anyway, but I soon came to regret this shortcut. Strawberry plants proved to be particularly sensitive to the applied minerals, quickly dying back beyond what's normal for our winter garden (although new leaves did regrow in a timely manner, so all was not lost). In contrast, garlic and overwintering herbs didn't seem to be affected by my oversight. Still, if you've got a choice, it's better to be safe than sorry—skip any living plants when remineralizing, then be sure to mark your garden map so you can hit those sites next year.

While I'm on the topic of remineralization mistakes, I feel obliged to inform you about the other disadvantages of my own campaign. I remineralized our entire garden in early March 2013, which cost us a couple of hundred dollars and a few gallons of strawberries. I was hoping to see higher yields and tastier vegetables in the years to come, but I have to admit that I've been unable to pick out any discernible effects of the remineralization campaign. The added nutrients probably didn't hurt and they might have helped, but would I do it again? Probably not. Unless faced with a serious deficiency in my soil, I'd be more likely to stick to annual applications of organic matter to bring the ground back into balance the natural way, perhaps combined with the biological remineralization techniques outlined in the next chapter.

Chapter 13:
Biological Methods of
Nutrient Balancing

Remineralization with Animals

We were surprised when this newly cleared pasture didn't immediately grow up in tall weeds. Was there a problem with the soil?

Although my experiences suggested that remineralizing already acceptable soil wasn't worth the expenditure of time and money, I soon found a plot of land that failed chapter 1's growability test and needed additional TLC. This area came into production in the winter of 2012/2013 when my husband and I expanded our core homestead out in a new direction to allow us to fence additional pastures. We cut down some trees, built an animal shelter . . . and watched as nothing grew.

When faced with a major lack of growability, I actually look at everything *except* pH and mineral imbalances first. Instead, it's handy to consider limiting factors, a concept that basically means ailing plants are lacking at least one environmental factor that they really need in order to reach peak productivity. For example, if only a single species is ailing while other types of plants do well in a given spot, the gardener might be dealing with improper heat, cold, or growing-season length for that species (or with pests and diseases). On the other hand, a more general lack of growability is often due to too little light or water, or perhaps to excessively harsh sunlight or overly swampy conditions.

Although not technically a limiting factor on plant growth, lack of growability may also be due to allelopathy. Many of you are probably already familiar with the fact that black walnut trees produce a toxic substance—juglone—in their leaves and roots. Although some plants can handle the natural toxin, others dwindle and then die when faced with juglone-tainted soil. Similarly, species beyond walnuts can be allelopathic as well, with ailanthus (a.k.a. tree of heaven) being another major player in this regard. In fact, even some common garden plants can have allelopathic effects on subsequent crops, with sorghum, rye, wheat, oilseed radishes, sunflowers, buckwheat, broccoli, and peas all having at least some tendencies in that direction.

In the case of my problematic pasture, I considered and rejected both allelopathy and the common limiting factors mentioned above, which led me to the conclusion that the area actually *was* suffering from a soil-related issue. My first guess was that there wasn't enough nitrogen to go around, since new garden plots often lack this essential nutrient and since nitrogen-fixing trees dominated the area (a clue that non-nitrogen-fixers were too starved to compete). Since I had a solid hypothesis about what was wrong, I decided to skip the soil test and instead pastured a round of summer broilers on the poor ground to see what would happen.

We asked twenty Australorp broilers to help boost the nitrogen levels of our poorest pasture. The chickens were willing, but the soil still failed to cooperate.

In case you're planning to follow suit, the average full-grown layer applies about 2.5 pounds of nitrogen, 0.6 pounds of phosphorus, and 0.9 pounds of potassium to the soil over the course of a year. In contrast, an heirloom broiler, raised from chick to freezer over the course of four months, will instead apply roughly 0.4 pounds of nitrogen, 0.1 pounds of phosphorus, and 0.1 pounds of potassium per year. So my twenty heirloom broilers ranging over 1600 square feet were providing the equivalent of 200 pounds of nitrogen fertilizer and 54 pounds of both potassium and phosphorus per acre. In other words, their manure alone should have been sufficient to jump-start plant growth if lack of nitrogen was the soil's only problem.

Unfortunately, weed growth still lagged behind in this pasture despite our chickens' hard work, so I finally plunked down the cash for a soil test. The results were distressing. Even post-chickens, the pasture's pH clocked in at an ultra-acidic 5.2, while cation exchange capacity was a distressingly low 7. There were other soil deficiencies in play as well, although those nutrient imbalances could have simply been side effects of the low organic matter and pH.

While assessing my soil-test results, I also took a closer look at the lay of the land. Aerial photos from the 1950s showed that this and other parts of our core homestead had been cleared for row crops and pasture half a century ago, and it soon became clear that those previous farmers had lacked an understanding of how essential it is not to plow ground in the fall and leave fields fallow over the winter. As a result of this and similar management choices, topsoil soon eroded away to form vast gullies on either side of what would become my new pasture. In other words, I wasn't trying to create a pasture out of forest-turned-homestead; I was trying to grow edibles atop poor subsoil where all of the topsoil had long since eroded away. No wonder even weeds failed to thrive.

Given that information, a smart farmer would have limed the heck out of the impoverished pasture, then perhaps considered a remineralization campaign to bring other imbalances back into line. I instead decided to see what a second type of animal would do about my soil problem. I talked my husband into letting me bring home a pair of small milk goats, then we proceeded to feed the does with copious off-farm hay and kelp plus on-farm weeds and cover crops. I didn't expect our does to get much (if any) nutrition from the few plants growing in their poor pasture, but our livestock *did* spend most of their days there, depositing goat "berries" and urine. Would ruminant manure be sufficient, I wondered, to repair decades of human neglect?

Chloritic comfrey proved that our soil continued to have major problems even after a chicken-pasturing campaign.

Sure enough, by the subsequent summer, plants were slowly beginning to grow in what had previously been almost-barren ground. No, this pasture hasn't yet become the vibrant jungle you'll see in other parts of our core homestead, and our dainty nannies aren't yet deigning to dine on their own pasture weeds. But the influx of goat manure has already turned the tables on soil that had failed to rebound in the half century since it had last been farmed.

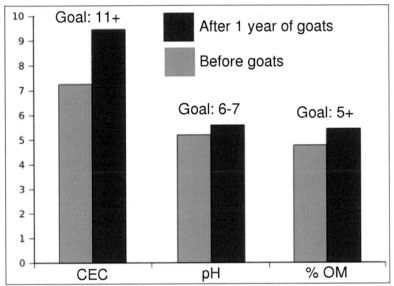

One year of goat manure had a remarkable effect on the pasture's poor soil.

To me, the increase in plant growability told me everything I needed to know about the pasture's soil improvement. But, for the sake of this book, I decided to send away a second soil sample to be analyzed after a year of goat grazing. The changes were striking. In twelve months with no additional amendments, CEC in the pasture had increased by 30%, organic matter levels had improved by 14%, and pH had risen from 5.2 to 5.6. Meanwhile, nutrient imbalances elsewhere in the soil also seemed to be correcting themselves. Calcium levels increased from 33% of the base saturation to 42%, drawing closer to the 60 to 70% figures recommended by remineralization advocates. Overall, I figure our two small goats will have this pasture up to par in another year or two . . . while providing our family with milk and meat in the process.

The take-home message from this section is—you can provide many of the same effects of pH balancing and remineralization by simply grazing animals over the problematic ground. And even though I found the changes in my pasture startling, this is far from a new idea. In fact, before the advent of chemical fertilizers, European farmers used a cycle of fallowing (often in the form of a temporary meadow called a ley) to regenerate their garden soil. The farmers would begin by growing vegetables on a plot of land for perhaps four or five years until production began to decline, then the area was seeded to grasses and legumes for a similar length of time. If the farmers were lucky enough to own animals, the livestock grazed on the ley during the fallow period as well, thus rebuilding fertility and soil structure through the actions of both plant roots and animal manure.

More recently, farmers have been noting measurable improvements in both soil quality and animal health using modern pasture-rotation systems. Pigs and poultry are good choices for renovating ground that may be low in macronutrients but is otherwise in good shape since their simple stomachs produce manure high in nitrogen, phosphorus, and potassium. On the other hand, ruminants like cows, goats, and sheep really carry the day when it comes to overall soil improvement since these species eat tough plant matter and produce fibrous manure that boosts soil organic-matter levels while also increasing nutrient concentrations in the ground. Horses, rabbits, llamas, and alpacas can digest moderately fibrous plant matter, so these species' effects on a pasture lie in between the other two extremes.

Of course, if your soil is really poor, you won't be able to feed livestock from problematic pastures and will be forced to bring in hay to round out their diets as we did. But John Seymour's classic *The Self-Sufficient Life and How to Live It* makes a strong case for buying off-farm feed while bringing your farm's fertility back into balance. Seymour posits that the effects of passing hay through a ruminant are much greater than you'd obtain by simply spreading that same hay over problematic ground, and my results have supported his hypothesis. Perhaps the additional boost comes from beneficial microorganisms present in your goat, cow, or sheep manure?

Photo credit: Greg Judy, www.greenpasturesfarm.net

Greg Judy uses mob grazing to improve poor pastures quickly while applying no purchased soil amendments.

Homesteaders with lots of land at their fingertips will see equally impressive results by simply passing herds of beef cattle across poor ground in quick bursts of high-density grazing. Mob-grazing expert Greg Judy begins by feeding cows for a year using hay applied directly on top of poor soil, figuring whatever isn't eaten will be worked into the ground while also seeding grasses and legumes to provide next year's pasture crop. During the following growing season, he continues to renovate poor pasture areas, this time by turning large quantities of animals into long, skinny areas to trample unpalatable weeds at the same time as the ruminants gorge on the cream of the pasture crop. In general, Judy's goal is to see 60% of the plant matter in a pasture eaten, 30% trampled into the soil, and 10% left standing to protect the ground. Then—usually after a day or less—animals are moved off that portion of pasture and are not allowed to return to the previously grazed spot until grasses are just starting to develop a seed head (the so-called boot stage). Using this type of pasture management, Judy has noticed dramatic increases in soil quality and in earthworm numbers every year . . . along with healthy cattle that thrive in his high-intensity system.

Of course, most of you probably don't have the acreage and infrastructure to follow Greg Judy's approach. I don't either. But a couple of goats, a hutch of rabbits, or even simply committing to hauling in manure from a neighbor's farm can work wonders in improving the most problematic of soils. Just keep an eye on sodium levels if your climate doesn't have enough rain to flush excess salts away, and make sure your animals stay healthy with off-farm feeds if necessary. Then you'll be remineralizing and rebalancing soil while feeding your family in the process.

Boosting Phosphorus with Fungi

I've now written about multiple ways of improving soils deficient in most of the major macro- and micronutrients. But you'll notice that I adroitly sidestepped any mention of phosphorus even though most farmers consider this one of the top three most important nutrients for plant growth. The trouble is that phosphorus is usually present in sufficient quantities in soil, but the mineral may nonetheless be virtually inaccessible to your plants. In fact, unlike many other nutrients that move through soil so easily that they're leached away in every heavy rain, phosphorus stays put almost too well. So if your soil is dry, cold, or compacted . . . good luck getting any phosphorus into your plants' roots no matter how much is present in the soil!

Mycorrhizal fungi that team up with crop plants generally produce small, underground fruiting bodies that gardeners are unlikely to notice. But tree-friendly mycorrhizal fruits include many of the beautiful mushrooms that pop up on the forest floor after spring and fall rains.

Chemical farmers get around this issue by pouring on more phosphorus fertilizer every year. They're also careful to manage soil pH to promote phosphorus availability since the nutrient is significantly less available to plants at a pH lower than 6 or higher than 7. I don't recommend this traditional approach, but if you want to take the phosphorus-fertilization shortcut, organic sources include bone meal, chicken manure, and finely ground rock phosphate.

You don't really need these phosphorus-heavy amendments, though, because there's a much simpler (and cheaper) solution. In the wild, plants are able to uptake sufficient phosphorus as the result of a partnership with microscopic fungi known as mycorrhizae. The mycorrhizal fungi in essence extend plant roots into much more distant and smaller cracks in the soil matrix than the host plants could ever dream of colonizing on their own. In the process, fungi suck up hard-to-find phosphorus along with other plant-friendly minerals like zinc and copper. Then, as a thank you for the mycorrhizae's hard work, the host plants feed their mycorrhizal partners with plenty of sugars that fungi couldn't readily create on their own.

In addition to the food exchange, mycorrhizal fungi also help their plant buddies by sucking up water during drought conditions, by helping stave off soil-borne diseases, and by making toxic levels of aluminum and heavy metals less dangerous to sensitive plants. Finally, mycorrhizal fungi improve conditions for future generations by secreting glues known as glomalin that are extremely effective in soil aggregation. The short version is—you really want mycorrhizae in your garden soil because these fungi are your crops' best friends. In fact, laboratory experiments in which plants are grown in sterile media prove that lack of mycorrhizae leads to very poor plant growth, so these fungal partners are more of a must-have than icing on the cake.

So I'm telling you to shell out the cash for mycorrhizal inoculants no matter the cost, right? Not unless you plan to garden on Mars. Most of us will find that mycorrhizal fungi quickly colonize our gardens with no inoculation necessary as soon as we stop using traditional farming techniques that caused these plant partners to perish. The trouble is that mycorrhizal fungi are particularly sensitive to tilling and to bare soil, and they also tend to dwindle in soils excessively high in phosphorus. But if you use no-till gardening techniques, keep the soil surface sheltered by mulch or cover crops, and don't pour on fertilizers you don't really need, fungi will proliferate, helping your crops suck up the nutrients and water necessary for optimal growth.

Cover Crops

From a soil-conditioning and weed-control standpoint, grains are your best cover-crop choice. I'm a big fan of oats planted in August because the grassy stalks quickly outcompete all weeds, the plants naturally winter-kill in our zone-6 climate, and the cover crop leaves a light layer of mulch behind to protect the soil of our winter garden. Oh, and our goats love grazing on the crop tops too.

So both animals and fungi are extremely effective at improving soil. Do plants bring anything special to the table?

Cover crops answer that question with a resounding yes. These plants are grown for the express purpose of improving soil, and they do the job dramatically, increasing organic matter levels, creating biopores, and reducing weed pressure.

However, with a few exceptions, I recommend against expecting plants to be a quick fix for extremely poor or imbalanced soil. Instead it's best to count on these handy crops to bring good soil to the next level of excellence or to maintain already top-notch earth.

The trouble with using cover crops during the early stages of soil improvement is that even the hardest-working plant requires a certain bare minimum soil condition in order to thrive. And if cover crops don't thrive, then they won't be able to do much to help your soil improve. So you're better off relieving major soil problems first, then turning to plants to do the final job of conditioning before (or in between) growing vegetables for the table.

My own adventures with cover cropping began when I attended a biochar workshop in 2010 . . . and came home with a bee in my bonnet about buckwheat. Since then, I've tried out at least a dozen species and have developed a focus on a few cover crops that I believe will turn most home gardens into a near-instant success. I've written extensively about the nitty gritty of using cover crops to maintain a no-till garden in my book *Homegrown Humus*, so I won't repeat that information here. But I do want to spend a few more minutes selling you on the concept since buckwheat, oats, oilseed radishes, rye, and soybeans have become a staple in my own garden campaign.

What's the big deal about cover crops? Gardeners typically see so much improvement for so little expenditure of time and money that the technique feels a bit like the humus equivalent of a get-rich-quick scheme. On our own farm, I've noticed startling increases in soil organic-matter levels since I began planting buckwheat in gaps in the summer garden and using other crops to keep the ground active during the winter months. Fall-planted oats in particular have proven to be a key component of my anti-weed campaign, preventing those pesky chickweed and dead-nettle plants from spreading their seeds during the off season and swallowing up our spring garden.

Nitrogen-fixing nodules attached to the roots of leguminous cover crops are home to bacteria that suck nitrogen out of the air and make that important nutrient available to plants. In this category, soybeans and cowpeas are good choices for adding nitrogen to a no-till garden since they're both easy to kill. For maximum soil improvement, pull up legumes just as the plants begin to create their first seed pods since older plants move most of their nutrients out of stems, leaves, and roots to sock the goodies away in their seeds.

I was also surprised to find that areas treated to a winter cover crop showed increased seedling survival rates the next spring compared to areas put to bed beneath a heavy layer of straw. Honestly, I'd mostly turned to winter cover crops to save my back and wallet since purchased winter mulches are energetically and financially expensive. But I soon came to realize that the so-called living soil food web—consisting of microbes that cluster around growing roots to swap nutrients back and forth with plants—fades back to the bare minimum during a sleepy garden winter. On the other hand, if I keep living plants active on that plot of earth for most of the off-season, then populations of important soil microbes remain copious and active, ready to team up with the first lettuce and broccoli seedlings so my veggies will take off as soon as the ground is warm enough to work.

Buckwheat is my go-to cover crop during short gaps in the summer garden. The grain begins blooming thirty days after planting, at which point I yank up clumps of cover crop and lay the plants across dry garden soil to die in the sun. The tender buckwheat will have melted back into the ground within a few weeks, or you can rake the buckwheat "mulch" to the side of the bed after only a day or two to plant into the bare soil immediately. Those of you with larger gardening plots will also find it easy to kill buckwheat by mowing, scything, or weed-eating the plants near the soil surface.

The benefits of cover crops in the home garden don't stop there. You can put erosion in your rearview mirror once cover crops become a normal part of your planting cycle, and pollinators also thrive when they have buckwheat blossoms to sip from next door to your vegetable flowers. Leguminous cover crops increase the amount of nitrogen in your soil, and all cover crops keep nitrogen cycling so the nutrient doesn't wash away during fallow-season rains.

Oilseed radishes are a good autumn choice if you want to be able to plant into the same area in the very early spring. As long as you garden in USDA zone 6 or colder, the radish cover crop will perish on its own around midwinter, completely rotting away by the time the ground is warm enough to plant the first lettuce or peas. In the meantime, the long, thick taproot leaves behind biopores that soften up deep layers of your soil, leading to the alternative moniker "tillage radish."

Last, but not least, I have to admit that garden visitors are instantly drawn to broad swathes of cover crops. My mother is always begging to eat my oilseed radishes, and beds of blooming buckwheat buzz with insect life in the early morning air.

How much does all of this ecosystem bounty cost? We spend less than $30 per year on cover-crop seeds for our half-acre garden, and that involves huge swathes of oats planted primarily for winter goat fodder. A dinner out for two, or a whole year of garden improvement—you decide which is a better use of your cash.

Dynamic Accumulators

Comfrey is one of the best-known dynamic accumulators. But does this species actually pull up hard-to-find minerals out of the subsoil, or is comfrey simply a heavy feeder of nutrients already available in the upper layer of the earth?

I could sing the praises of cover crops all day long, but I have to admit that I've slowly come to the realization that the other major category of plant soil-improver—dynamic accumulators—is more wish than reality. If you haven't heard the term before, dynamic accumulators are plants that are believed to delve deep into the soil to mine usually inaccessible nutrients, concentrating those found minerals in their leaves and roots. Various books recommend that gardeners gather the tops to create high-nutrient compost, or simply site dynamic accumulators next door to more needy crops so the former's organic matter can be allowed to rot into the ground and improve upper layers of the soil for the sake of the latter. In other words, dynamic accumulators have the potential to join the ranks of ruminants and mycorrhizae, improving extremely poor ground so that edibles can then be grown in the enriched earth.

The trouble with this rosy picture is that scientific analyses of the effects of dynamic accumulators are scanty and tend to contradict the common belief expounded upon in the previous paragraph. In *Understanding Roots*, for example, Robert Kourik uses data from real-life excavations to prove that most so-called dynamic accumulators merely concentrate nutrients already found in the topsoil rather than digging deep for scanty minerals. To prove this point, he turns to a variety of root maps that show the lack of deep roots in most dynamic accumulator species. For example, comfrey (a classic dynamic accumulator that is believed to concentrate silica, calcium, nitrogen, magnesium, potassium, and iron) actually keeps most of its roots in the top foot of soil. This is the same zone used by crop plants due to the fact that topsoil contains peak nutrient levels, plenty of oxygen, and lots of beneficial microorganisms. Kourik asserts that deeper roots in both comfrey and in other plants are much less prolific than have been previously believed and that the few taproots that exist seem to function as anchors and as a way to suck up water during droughts rather than as seekers of plant nutrients.

I don't recommend planting comfrey beneath young fruit trees since the dynamic accumulator will steal nitrogen from your tree's roots. The yellow leaves on this nectarine are a classic sign of nitrogen deficiency.

My own experience has backed up Kourik's assertions. Before I knew any better, I planted comfrey in a ring a foot or so away from the trunk of a young nectarine tree. After a few years, the comfrey had completely covered the ground beneath the tree's canopy . . . and appeared to be outcompeting the nectarine for every important soil nutrient. Specifically, yellowing tree leaves proved that comfrey was particularly adept at accumulating nitrogen, not from deep in the soil profile but from the same zone where the nectarine roots were hunting this important nutrient. In the end, I concluded that comfrey (and perhaps other dynamic accumulators) are only worth planting near fruit trees once the latter are large enough to keep the former in line with heavy shade.

So which dynamic accumulators do I recommend growing for soil-conditioning purposes beyond simple organic-matter production? The nitrogen-fixers are an obvious choice since these plants team up with bacteria to pull nitrogen out of the air, eventually releasing that nutrient into the soil to feed future crops. But otherwise, I recommend letting go of the belief that you can use dynamic accumulators to remineralize your soil. Instead, it's best to either follow the chemical route or to focus on animals and fungi to relieve paucities. Then, once your basic deficiencies have been brought into balance, you can start planting cover crops to really boost that moderate soil and turn your growing area into black gold.

ORGANIC SOIL AMENDMENTS

Choosing the best types of organic matter for each garden situation keeps plants healthy and fruits tasty.

Although there are many other solutions to problematic soil, you've probably gathered by now that my all-around favorite soil-improvement strategy is to boost organic-matter levels. As a result, the remainder of this book has been devoted to conventional and not-so-conventional ways of adding organic matter back into impoverished soil or otherwise keeping your garden in tip-top health.

But while every amendment listed is helpful, you'll have best results choosing from the menu based on your own garden's needs. After all, organic amendments have a variety of purposes in the garden, ranging from rich fertilizers that release day-to-day nitrogen that your plants crave through mulches that block out weeds, hold in water, and keep microorganisms happy. Meanwhile, other sources of organic matter are added to a garden for the primary purpose of improving the soil quality over the long term, even though they might cause short-term stunting in crops when microorganisms steal nitrogen from elsewhere in the soil to help them decompose the woodier debris. So in an effort to make these final chapters easier to access, I've summarized the primary purpose of each amendment in the table below.

Primary purpose of organic soil amendments

Amendment	Fertilization	Mulch	Soil Conditioning
Cover crops	X	X	X
Conventional compost	X		X
Bokashi compost	X		X
Worm castings	X		X
Black-soldier-fly castings	X		
Compost tea	X		X
Animal manure	X		X
Deep bedding	X	X	X
Humanure	X	X	X
Urine	X		
Biodynamic preparation 500	X		X

Amendment	Fertilization	Mulch	Soil Conditioning
Wood chips, sawdust, and shavings		X	X
Rotting logs			X
Stump dirt			X
Cardboard		X	
Paper		X	
Biochar			X
Ashes	X		
Straw		X	X
Hay and grass clippings	X	X	X
Chop 'n drop	X	X	X
Tree leaves		X	X
Seaweed and algae	X	X	X
Food scraps and coffee grounds	X		
Peat, coco- nut coir, and humates			X

But don't start adding cardboard mulches and horse-manure compost to your garden just yet. First, let's take a step back and delve a little deeper into the biology and chemistry of organic matter so you'll fully understand which amendments will be the best fit for your plot of earth.

Chapter 14:
Choosing Amendments
with Biology in Mind

Tracking Down Humus

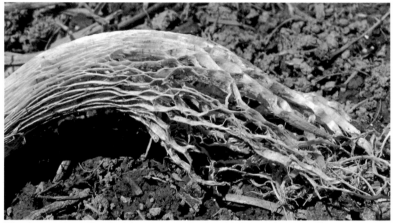

Woody organic matter that decomposes slowly adds humus to your soil.

The first factor you should consider when choosing garden amendments is—which type of organic matter will I be adding to my soil? I introduced the concept of different types of organic matter in chapter 4, where I made the distinction between active organic matter that will break down readily to feed your plants this year and passive organic matter that decomposes much more slowly and is primarily responsible for increasing soil quality. Here, I want to be a bit less scientific, so I'll use the term gardeners are more familiar with for the latter category—humus.

Although you'd be hard pressed to distinguish between these two types of organic matter with the naked eye, every experienced gardener will tell you that it's pretty easy to tell whether you've managed to track down humus because this amendment takes your gardening to the next level. Scientists like to add that humus contains most of the soil's nitrogen, boron, molybdenum, phosphorus, and sulfur. Meanwhile, the organic acids created when humus decays make phosphorus, zinc, and iron more available to plants, while also binding to and storing micronutrients so those minerals don't wash away during heavy rains. I guess those experienced gardeners were right—it's easy to tell if your soil is high in humus because plants growing there are huge, green, and vibrant from all those extra nutrients.

But if you can't tell the difference between active and passive organic matter with the naked eye, how can you tell that the compost you create or buy has plenty of humus in it? The trick is to understand the chemistry of humus formation. While any plant matter mixed with the proper amount of water and kept at the right temperature will eventually create compost, you need lignin-rich (tough and woody) plants combined with some source of nitrogen to create long-lived passive organic matter. This is why buckwheat cover crops—which seem soft and succulent at harvest time—tend to create primarily active organic matter that simply cycles the existing nutrients through the soil. In contrast, a rye cover crop—which is so tough at harvest time that the dead plant matter can actually steal some nitrogen from succeeding plantings—is more likely to boost your soil's humus levels. Similarly, hugelkultur is a great way to increase garden humus levels since wood is nearly 100% lignin. On the other hand, chicken manure is rich in immediately available nutrients but provides little or no long-term improvement to the soil.

Although you may not be familiar with the word "lignin," most gardeners know where this woody plant part is present—at the tough bases of asparagus shoots and broccoli heads or in okra pods that have stayed on the plant a little too long.

I know this section is veering awfully close to the "I can't see it with my eyes, so why should I care?" line, so let me make it simpler for you. You may have never heard the term lignin before, but your taste buds know exactly what I'm talking about. Have you ever snapped off the bases of asparagus stalks and dropped them onto the compost pile because you knew those butts would turn stringy and hard to chew when cooked? Or perhaps you've decided not to harvest okra that's more than a day or two old because the bigger pods are also tough and inedible? If so, then you're discarding the lignin.

In general, if the materials you compost could be easily eaten by humans or chickens, then they have nearly no lignin present and are unlikely to break down into humus. On the other hand, if the materials being composted would make your goats or rabbits happy, then they contain a small to moderate amount of lignin and will probably create a nice combination of active and passive organic matter. Finally, if only termites or mushrooms would be able to eat your composta-bles, then the materials are 100% lignin and will rot slowly into soil-improving humus.

A happy garden will be fed compost consisting of a good ratio of all three levels of lignin because the resulting amend-ment will contain enough active organic matter to feed plants today plus enough passive organic matter to keep the soil itself happy. As with life, balance and moderation is key to a healthy garden. So aim for both active and passive organic matter if you want to make your vegetables thrive.

Fungi versus Bacteria

You can't see soil bacteria with your naked eye, but fungi are visible as whitish threads running through woody mulches.

Another important distinction to consider as you choose the proper amendments for your soil is which decomposing microorganisms are being fed with the compost application. The reason this is important is because active organic mat-ter doesn't miraculously feed your plants and passive organic matter doesn't miraculously improve your soil. Both amendments require the help of microbes to reach your desired objective, and the type of microorganisms you promote with your gardening tactics will impact everything from which plants thrive where to whether any humus ends up improving the tilth of your ground.

I'll start with bacteria because these microorganisms are the most abundant in traditional farm fields. Bacteria are among the smallest critters in your soil, so they do well with small soil pores found in poorly aggregated soil. These microorganisms also thrive in well-aerated soil, so their populations explode after tilling, making lots of nitrogen and sulfur immediately available for plant use. Unfortunately, bacteria have major shortfalls in the decomposition department. They can't handle acidic conditions, they don't create humus, and they really want their environment to be at least 70 degrees Fahrenheit in order to thrive. This is why those of you who till your garden will probably have to turn to seed meals to get nutrients to your plants in early spring—fungi aren't around due to previous episodes of soil churning, and the bacteria present are all huddled up in their winter coats, too chilly to do the job of creating plant-friendly nitrogen.

In contrast, no-till gardeners are instead promoting fungi (although bacteria will still make up around half of our soil microorganisms). These microscopic relatives of the mushroom are very handy to have around, but they can't stand plowing because they don't like their long strands getting broken apart. In addition, fungi also require large pores that form in well-aggregated soil but that are torn up by tilling. On the other hand, fungi thrive when gardeners add lignin-rich materials to their soil, especially if the organic matter is deposited on the surface rather than being mixed into the ground. Jump through all of these hoops, and you'll end up with all the benefits of fungally dominated soil—mycorrhizal partnerships, well-aggregated particles, and loads of humus. Plus, decomposition will take place even during cold weather and in soggy or acidic soil, so you'll have fewer problems with starving plants in the early spring. That's why it's worth keeping fungi happy, especially if you're growing woody plants like fruit trees that thrive in fungally dominated soil.

While the distinction between fungi and bacteria is really enough for the average gardener to understand, I can't resist mentioning one other type of microorganism. Actinomycetes are technically bacteria but they act more like fungi, aiding in decomposition and humus formation and working even at relatively low temperatures. And unlike most bacteria, it's easy to tell whether actinomycetes are present in your dirt because they produce that rich, woodsy aroma that many gardeners associate with prime compost or with leaf mold on the forest floor. These microorganisms have their own niche in the earth, too, decomposing organic matter even during drought conditions and also creating antibiotics that protect plant roots from harmful pathogens. Sound good? Then add lots of ruminant manure to your garden since this amendment is particularly good at promoting actinomycete populations.

Finally, I can't leave the topic of microorganisms before mentioning that most of these microscopic critters stick very close to the earth's surface. And, as a result, most plant feeder roots stay in the top inch of soil as well. So even though you might notice a long tap root on a vegetable plant, you should be aware that your crops are depending primarily on the thin skin of microbially-rich dirt in front of your eyes. In order to help plants take advantage of the area they care about the most, you should mulch, water, and weed well to ensure that your root zone is full of fungi, bacteria . . . and vegetable roots too!

C:N Ratio

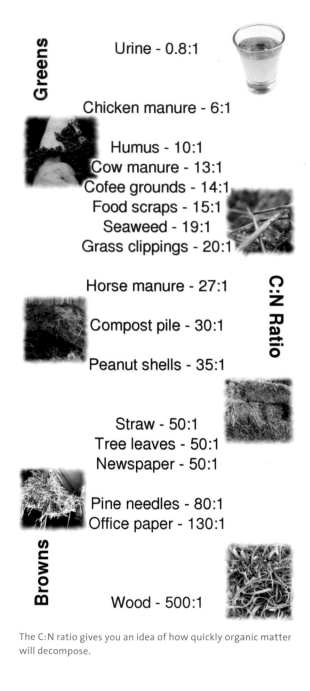

Greens

Urine - 0.8:1

Chicken manure - 6:1

Humus - 10:1
Cow manure - 13:1
Cofee grounds - 14:1
Food scraps - 15:1
Seaweed - 19:1
Grass clippings - 20:1

Horse manure - 27:1

Compost pile - 30:1

Peanut shells - 35:1

Straw - 50:1
Tree leaves - 50:1
Newspaper - 50:1

Pine needles - 80:1
Office paper - 130:1

Browns

Wood - 500:1

C:N Ratio

The C:N ratio gives you an idea of how quickly organic matter will decompose.

The final big-picture topic I want to cover before delving into individual organic-matter sources is the carbon-to-nitrogen ration (often abbreviated C:N). Those of you who hate math are probably tuning me out already, but please stick around for another minute or two! If you've ever built a compost pile, you already understand this concept since you mentally separated organic matter into browns and greens in the process. The C:N ratio is just a way of putting numbers to that distinction so it's easier to keep the greenness or brownness of materials in line.

As you can see from the chart on the previous page, a well-built compost pile has a C:N of about 30:1, which is a bit like the neutral 7 on the pH scale. Below this value, most materials will rot too quickly on their own to feed your garden and its associated microorganisms properly. That's why if you mound up a lot of chicken manure without any straw bedding, you smell that foul ammonia odor, a sign that nitrogen is being lost to the air rather than sticking around to feed your crops. The solution? Mix in some browns of course!

Meanwhile, good mulches tend to have a C:N of around 50:1. This level is a little woodier than a perfect compost pile, which means the mulch materials resist decomposition for at least a few months to block weeds and hold in moisture around your plant roots. But 50:1 mulches aren't so high in difficult-to-decompose organic matter that microorganisms are forced to steal nitrogen from the surrounding soil in order to get the rotting process moving, making them pretty safe to apply even around seedlings. That said, it's better not to mix straw, tree leaves, and cut cover crops directly into your soil unless you add a higher nitrogen amendment like compost or manure at the same time. Alternatively, you can get around the initial nitrogen loss during early decomposition by waiting a few weeks between application and planting, a process which gives soil microorganisms a head start on the woodier debris before organic matter is expected to feed your crops.

At the far extreme, fresh wood products like sawdust, wood chips, or logs will definitely act as nitrogen sinks in the soil, at least initially. Gardeners deal with this issue by allowing woody materials to decompose for several months before application, by adding high-nitrogen amendments (like urine or chicken manure) during the decomposition process, and by either burying the wood considerably below your crop's roots (such as in hugelkultur) or by applying the materials only to the soil surface (as in mulch).

Okay, enough of the numbers. Let's take a look at some top-notch sources of organic matter and how I recommend using each in your garden.

Chapter 15: Compost

Conventional Compost

Building a compost pile can be as simple as piling up a lot of organic matter and waiting for it to rot.

The traditional organic gardener's approach to increasing humus levels is applying compost. In a perfect world, this amendment contains a good proportion of both passive and active organic matter and has been allowed to heat to a high enough temperature to kill all weed seeds. Adding between half and one inch of this amendment to the top of your garden soil before each crop will result in the perfect garden we all dream of.

The trouble with this rosy picture is that it's beyond the reach of most serious gardeners to come up with enough organic matter to create homegrown compost to feed all of their crops. I figure that my husband and I need about 8 cubic yards of finished compost annually just to feed our vegetable garden, not to mention our woody perennials. Since compostables usually reduce to at least a quarter of their original volume as they decompose, that means my compost pile would begin life at four feet high and fifteen feet square. That's one big compost pile!

Luckily, there are lots of less traditional ways to feed your garden, which I'll outline in later sections. But in case you *do* want to build a compost pile, here are a few tips to get you started. First of all, the optimal size is about five feet square and four feet high since this will allow the center to heat up naturally without being beyond the average human's ability to turn. In a perfect world, you'd mix lignin-rich materials (like tree leaves or summer weeds) with high-nitrogen materials (like food scraps or spring lawn clippings) and add just enough water to keep your pile cooking nicely. If you feel like the compost is becoming too wet, you probably need to add more woody materials (like tree leaves); if the pile feels too dry, you probably need more nitrogen (which I add in the form of pee). Finally, don't forget to cover your compost pile once it's about halfway decomposed if you live in a rainy climate since uncovered compostables will lose much of their nitrogen to leaching before you add the precious amendment to your garden.

"Wait a minute—don't I need a bin?" the new gardener may ask. There are dozens of different types of compost bins on the market, but most of you won't need anything so fancy. From a utilitarian standpoint, bins are primarily useful for keeping critters out of food scraps and for holding your compost pile together so it decomposes faster. You can get the same results with a homemade bin made of stacked cinderblocks or wired-together pallets.

On the other hand, tumblers that you turn with a crank do add value by making compost faster. If you're on a budget (or want to produce more compost than will fit into a tumbler), you can get the same effect by using a pitchfork to rearrange the pile's contents, moving the edges to the center and vice versa a few weeks after the pile is first built. Or, if you're not too concerned about weed seeds, you can just take the slow, lazy approach of letting your pile mellow in situ until it's done.

Those bin purposes aside, I think most gardeners purchase a bin for aesthetic reasons. If you're an urban homesteader trying to make your edible garden fit into a classy neighborhood, you'll definitely need a bin, either found, made, or bought.

When purchasing compost, pay attention to the ingredients that make up the piles. This warehouse uses bedding from an industrial chicken facility to produce high-nitrogen compost.

And then, once you realize you need much more compost than will fit in your tumbler, it's time to look for sources further afield. Store-bought compost comes in many shapes and sizes, and the savvy shopper will focus on which ingredients made up each producer's pile. Municipal compost is often a good choice since autumn leaves and chipped branches increase the humus content, although the possibility of heavy metals and other pollutants is present. Compost from large chicken farms is another alternative, with the plus that the finished product is very high in nitrogen but with the minus that chicken-manure compost doesn't provide the same long-term soil improvement as less rich materials.

But even composted chicken manure is preferable to the "compost" you buy in bags at the big-box store. Bagged compost always strikes me as microbially dead, and the product often seems to be mixed with lots of soil, making the compost quite low in available nutrients as well. As a result, I recommend buying compost only if you can examine the product beforehand. And if you have a pickup truck, you'll be much better off focusing on producers that sell compost by the yard rather than by the bag.

I know this is a very short section about a very important topic. But I suspect that the average gardener has already learned everything she wants to know about compost by this point. If not, there are a variety of resources to choose from. One of the best (and definitely the cheapest) is Steve Solomon's *Organic Gardener's Composting*, which may be read for free in ebook form on Amazon. Or just build a pile and start feeling your way through the process by trial and error. The same focused attention to detail that makes vegetables thrive will help you product top-notch compost in your own backyard.

Bokashi Compost

Gardeners who want to move beyond the traditional compost pile have several options to choose from. One of the currently trendy choices is bokashi, a type of container composting that began in Asia but has since been perfected and proprietized by Dr. Teruo Higa. Higa's EM-1 mixture of microorganisms contains lactic-acid bacteria, yeasts, and purple non-sulfur bacteria that together are reputed to rapidly digest food scraps in a closed system while producing few or no foul odors. Apartment dwellers are particularly fond of the system since they can sock away months of compostables in sealed buckets, then apply the fermented scraps to the garden the next spring.

Bokashi composting uses microbial starters and gamma-seal buckets to ferment food scraps. Here, I'm applying a *Lactobacillus* newspaper starter produced using yogurt and molasses.

In the best-case scenario, bokashi advocates say you can plant into bokashi compost in as little as four weeks—two weeks spent fermenting scraps with microbial starters in a sealed bucket, then two weeks composting in a trench in the ground. At the end of this time period, you should see no discernible food scraps, just rich, brown dirt where you applied your bokashi compost to the garden.

In 2015, I set out to see if these claims had any merit. My experiment was only mildly scientific because our family creates barely enough food scraps to attain the goal of filling a bokashi bucket within three weeks, so I had to run my test buckets successionally rather than all at the same time. But I figured if bokashi's results were really as startling as the proponents claim, I should be able to see a difference even with such monkey wrenches as slightly different types of scraps and seasons thrown into my experimental protocol.

To that end, I bought gamma-seal lids ($11 apiece) to turn five-gallon buckets into air-tight containers, then I sought out two types of bokashi starter. First, I purchased so-called EM-1 bran starter ($17 for two pounds), a pound of which is sufficient to colonize a five-gallon bucket of food scraps. Meanwhile, I also created *Lactobacillus* newspaper, the lower-tech homemade starter that begins by draining the whey from active yogurt, mixing that liquid with an equal amount of molasses, and then diluting the aforementioned mixture to four times its original volume with water. I soaked newspapers in the *Lactobacillus* mixture, then placed the wet paper in an airtight baggie to ferment for two weeks, giving the bacteria time to fully colonize the paper substrate.

Now it was time to begin my experiment. In all three buckets, I began by adding about four inches of dry sawdust to the bottom of the container. This layer soaks up any liquid that oozes out of the rotting food so you don't end up with sodden compost. Next, I added a thin dusting of bokashi bran, one layer of newspaper, or nothing (depending on which experimental bucket I was filling). After that came a couple of inches of food scraps and another layer of starter (except in the control bucket). I used a plastic grocery bag on top of this initial layer, pounding the bag with my fist to mash the food into the starter and block out air. Then, as food scraps accumulated in my kitchen, I repeated this layering process until each bucket was completely full.

Store-bought bokashi
starter, 2 months in
the ground

Homemade *Lactobacillus*
starter, 3 months in
the ground

Control (no starter),
4 months in the ground

The results of my unscientific experiment suggested that neither store-bought nor homemade bokashi starters hastened decomposition.

I was initially impressed by the bokashi bran, which *did* seem to keep rotten smells down when I opened the bucket during the second week of food application. However, another round of experimentation during hotter summer weather proved that even bokashi bran wasn't sufficient to beat out foul odors when temperatures rose above the recommended 90 degrees Fahrenheit.

But the real test from a gardening perspective was the end result. Would bokashi compost decompose fully after only two weeks in the bucket and then some additional time in the ground? To find out, I dug three shallow trenches in my garden and marked the location as I buried the contents of each bucket. Then, a few months later, I came back to dig up my buried treasure.

The photos on the previous page show the results of my three experimental treatments. Since I had to fill buckets one at a time, roughly a month elapsed between the day when I buried the control compost and the day when I buried the *Lactobacillus* compost, then another month elapsed between burial of the *Lactobacillus* compost and the EM-1 bokashi. If the store-bought starter was as vibrant an inoculant as advertised, I would have expected the EM-1 bokashi to have caught up to the other treatments despite having only been in the ground for two months to the control's four. However, you'll notice that the photos instead appear to represent a time-lapse image of decomposition, with food scraps still apparent after two months in the EM-1 bokashi, with a brown layer of compost still visible after three months in the *Lactobacillus* bokashi, and with only the toughest duck egg shells still visible after four months in the control plot.

As you can guess, my conclusion is that neither store-bought bokashi starter nor homemade *Lactobacillus* starter are worth the expense. And I also warn against following some proponents' advice to simply sprinkle bokashi bran on your traditional compost pile as a microbial starter since the microorganisms involved depend upon anaerobic conditions and will quickly die in the high-oxygen environment of a good compost pile. The addition won't hurt, but you're wasting your time and money in the process.

That said, my husband and I *were* impressed by the gamma-seal lids, which did indeed block out odor in all three treatments after the buckets were closed. So if you live in a small space and need to save up your compost for a rainy day, gamma-seal lids might be worth the price . . . or maybe you'd be better off investing in a worm farm.

Worm Bins and Towers

Worm castings are a particularly high-quality source of both humus and beneficial bacteria.

While bokashi didn't quite make the cut for me, another value-added compost product has more potential—vermicompost, also known as worm castings or simply worm poop. The beauty of vermicompost is that, after being passed through the digestive tract of a redworm (*Eisenia fetida*), organic matter comes out very high in beneficial bacteria, plant growth promoters, micronutrients, and humus. In fact, worm castings are too rich to use in large quantities, with plants preferring no more than 20% of their growing zone to be made up of castings. As a result, a little bit of this potent amendment goes a long way.

I've written about how to set up and manage a small worm bin in my book *The Weekend Homesteader*, so I won't repeat that information here. Suffice it to say that even an apartment dweller can compost her food scraps right under the kitchen sink with little outlay of time and money. Then, if you choose to scale up beyond that simple setup, the rest of this chapter will help you get started with two less mainstream types of worm systems.

One option that I've read about but have yet to try is an in-garden worm farm known as a worm tower. To begin, simply drill holes in the bottom of a 4- or 6-inch-diameter, pale-colored PVC pipe, bury the tube vertically in the earth so about a foot lies below ground and the other half sticks up above the earth's surface, then top it all off with a plastic container with small holes poked in the bottom. This last element is meant to protect the worms from sun and flies while also allowing moderate amounts of moisture to drip down onto your composting scraps.

Once the worm tower is built, it's quite simple to use. Just add a layer of bedding (autumn leaves and straw are both good choices), a layer of food scraps, a layer of bedding, and so forth until the tower is full. In a perfect world, worms will decompose your scraps as fast as your kitchen produces broccoli skins and apple cores, so the tower never really fills up. In the meantime, the accumulating vermicompost at the bottom if the pipe is immediately available to nearby plants, topping up your soil's fertility in the process.

In their original setting of Australia, worm towers were usually seeded with redworms just like the wrigglers you'd buy to put in your under-the-sink worm bin. However, blog-reader Sarah Oler was concerned that introduced redworms would perish each winter in the cold, desert environment in Colorado. So she instead filled her tower with leaves and food scraps and waited for wild earthworms to come. The results were better than she'd imagined. "I am amazed at how quickly my worm population grew in the first year and the subsequent years," Sarah wrote. "Now my garden soil is full of them and I don't have to do anything to maintain them other than adding my biowaste."

Sarah Oler uses worm towers to encourage ordinary earthworms in her zone-5, Colorado garden.

Sarah loves the way her worm towers make composting a simple, in-garden affair. She reports no foul odors, no pests, and no need to turn her compost pile. Instead, she simply pulls out her towers once a year and either distributes the worm castings around the garden or uses the vermicompost to start seedlings.

The only negative she's found beyond the limited space in her towers is the process of summer scrap-dumping. "You have to fight your way through jungles of tomato plants to add your biowaste," Sarah reported. The sustainable, easy source of worm castings, though, is more than worth it.

A midscale worm bin is a great way to turn manure into high-quality compost.

But what if you have a lot more organic matter than you can stuff down a few in-garden towers? One option is to scale up the simple kitchen worm bin with the goal of providing for a larger percentage of your garden's needs. I began our mid-scale composting endeavor by reading Binet Payne's *Worm Cafe*, which details how one teacher built sufficient bins to turn her cafeteria's food waste into the perfect amendment for her school garden. My husband and I liked the idea so much that we followed Payne's lead, creating several worm bins that were four feet wide, eight feet long, and one or two feet deep. We drilled holes in the bottoms of our bins to allow adequate drainage, then we added a lid to shield worms from the sun.

Actually, we also created a false bottom on each bin so I could collect the precious worm tea that drains out of over-wet vermicompost, but this part of our experiment was a wash on the large scale so I don't recommend you mimic our design. Similarly, if I were doing it all over again, I'd sink my worm bins into the ground to keep the crawlers cooler during summer days and warmer during the winter nights since, in the end, deep freezes were what did in our experiment. Or, better yet, if you possess a basement that never freezes, that would be the optimal environment for a midscale vermicomposting endeavor.

Your next question might be—how in the world do I fill up such a large bin? We initially teamed up with our local middle school to collect their food waste, but I don't recommend you follow our lead in that department either. Unfortunately, cafeteria food in our neck of the woods is based on starches, oils, and highly processed ingredients, none of which our worms enjoyed. After unhappy worms forced us to throw in the towel in that department, we changed over to a horse-manure-and-straw mixture that was free for the taking at a nearby farm. As long as we allowed the manure to naturally heat and then cool for a few weeks before mixing in worms, this substrate led to much happier vermicomposting colonies which soon turned our manure into tiny black pellets of rich worm castings.

As I mentioned above, we eventually got out of the worm business when a series of winters descended into the negative teens Fahrenheit and killed off our worms. But the castings sure were good while they lasted, and I recommend the manure-style bin to anyone who lives in a warmer climate, has room for worms within a greenhouse, or otherwise thinks she can keep redworms from freezing during winter's cold.

One of these days, we may try again with a subterranean bin since I got quite a kick out of watching the earthworm ecosystem unfold before my eyes. My plants tell me they'd also like another dose of the amendment that is considered by many to be the best organic fertilizer around.

Black Soldier Fly Larvae

Black soldier fly larvae quickly consume high-nitrogen waste like food scraps and manure.

Like compost worms, black soldier fly larvae are often raised for the express purpose of composting food scraps quickly. But unlike worms, these fly larvae aren't very well known, so I'm going to write about their management in much more depth.

I'll start with the potential. Black soldier fly bins are a bit more of a niche on the homestead, and I recommend them only for those of you who keep poultry or fish. Why? Because the output of compost is relatively low (only about five pounds of finished compost per one hundred pounds of food waste), with the small quantity being a plus only for city-dwellers who don't have room for a large compost pile.

On the other hand, the high-protein larvae more than make up for the lack of garden fertility if you're raising livestock that can benefit from the addition of insect protein to their diets. In fact, that same one hundred pounds of food waste will turn into about twenty pounds of big, black larvae that your flock will gobble right up before begging for more, so black soldier flies are a no-brainer for the backyard chicken keeper.

The black-soldier-fly bin shown here has a six-gallon capacity, which felt too limited for even our very low-waste family.

Of course, your operation is likely to be a lot smaller than the 100-pound figure mentioned above, so you should only expect to feed a very moderate number of chickens from a household black soldier fly bin. The six-gallon bin shown above, for example, can handle two pounds of food scraps per day if managed optimally (or half to a third that amount in more ordinary hands), which results in enough larvae to provide the daily protein needs of one to three chickens. Add in some grain to round out the birds' diets, and your family could have a healthy, nearly self-sufficient flock providing an egg or two per day.

Be sure to add a continuous velcro barrier around the inside top of your bin or pupae will escape. Here, the larvae are crawling through the gap in our velcro barrier.

Before I write more about the critters inside, I want to spend a minute talking about the bin itself. If you read about black soldier fly bins on the Internet, the required characteristics seem extraordinarily complicated. But after spending a summer with a relatively inexpensive purchased bin (made by *Black Soldier Fly Blog*, but not currently available for sale), I've determined that the flies don't require such overbuilding.

What you definitely need is some kind of perforated pipe that begins at the bin surface and pops out the bottom of your container, allowing exudate (compost tea) to drain away after you flush the contents with water. (More on why and how you flush the bin later.) You also need a lid with openings large enough for an adult black soldier fly to flit inside, plus a line of velcro along the inside top of the bin to keep black-soldier-fly larvae from crawling out. Finally, a pipe near the top of the bin (but below the velcro barrier) should lead into a collection chamber where mature larvae will gather, making them easy to feed to your chickens without rooting through the whole bin in search of grubs.

This black soldier fly is laying her eggs on the drainpipe of my bin.

What don't you really need? The ramp that runs up the inside of most black soldier fly bins didn't appear to be necessary since I watched larvae climb directly up the vertical walls of the bin to find the collection pipe. The complicated two-tiered top with spots for cardboard egg-laying strips also seemed redundant since I watched female flies arrive and lay their eggs wherever they felt like it in the bin itself. And the ant-repelling moat made by filling a Rubbermaid bin lid with water apparently wasn't necessary either since I accidentally let our moat dry out and the bin wasn't overrun by ants.

On the other hand, if I were building my own contraption from scratch, I'd add a few features that aren't found in others' units. I repeatedly found adult black soldier flies stuck within our collection container, so I recommend drilling holes in the top of that add-on large enough for a fly to escape but too small for the larvae to crawl through. Next, I'd probably aim for a twenty-gallon capacity to make the bin easier to manage. And I'd definitely follow the lead of the builder of our bin and use a container with transparent walls since it was a lot of fun (and quite useful) to watch the larvae working and growing amid my compostables.

If these requirements sound too complicated, you can buy a premade black soldier fly bin online, but you'll need to shell out some serious cash. The only available brand at the time of this writing is Biopod, and their cheapest unit costs around $200 once you factor in shipping. So maybe it's worth tackling the DIY project after all.

Once you have a bin on hand, your next step is to seed that container with larvae. First, halfway fill the bin with partially rotted sawdust, then head out and hunt for flies. But before I tell you about the various methods you can use to put out the vacancy sign at your grub hotel, you need to know more about the critter you're trying to catch.

Hermetia ilucens, also known as the black soldier fly, is a small, wasp-like insect that spends most of its life in the larval stage. Within the United States, dependable wild populations can be found in zones 7 and warmer, with some people as far north as zone 5 reporting that they have wild black soldier flies visiting their yards. Here in the mountains of southwest Virginia (USDA zone 6), black soldier flies are definitely present in the wild because we frequently find their black, scaly larvae in our compost piles if we add an excessive amount of high-nitrogen materials and allow the compost to become too wet. That's a good way to tell whether you have this species in your area, in fact—just keep an eye out for the grubs when dealing with rather nasty organic waste.

You can sometimes find black soldier fly eggs under the lids of garbage bins.

That said, despite having wild populations around, I find adults particularly difficult to attract to new bins. You can begin trying to lure in wild flies once weather warms up, with April being the earliest you're likely to find any adults around (but later in the summer being more likely). Dried grains or chicken feed soaked in water and allowed to stand in a container until it ferments is supposed to be a good attractant, as is sour milk. An alternative if you already have one bin going is to use some of the leachate from that existing container, painting the black liquid around the inside of the new bin's lid to take advantage of the fact that black soldier flies are attracted to the odor of other members of their species. Finally, some people have good luck looking for the tiny white eggs beneath the lids of garbage cans since black soldier flies are often attracted to the foul odors inside and might lay their eggs nearby.

The easy way to seed your bin is to buy eggs, which cost us about $20 but can be hard to find online.

It wasn't very hard for me to track down some larvae that were nearly ready to pupate (having already turned black) beneath the bedding in our duck coop, but these larvae were apparently not sufficient to attract adult flies to our bin. As a result, I gave in and let my husband spend $20 ordering eggs online. This is the most dependable method of getting a bin going, but I have to admit it offends my self-sufficient sensibilities since you almost always have to start fresh every spring, and I found it no easier to lure in adult flies during our bin's second year.

Why not just keep the bin active all winter long? In the wild, members of the species spend the cold season in their pupal stage, so your bin will usually clear out on its own before heavy freezes hit. And even though many experimenters have theorized about winterizing bins so larvae remain active year-round, I've yet to hear from anyone north of Florida who has successfully kept their bins going through the winter.

Yellow soldier flies are related to black soldier flies and do a similar job, although this species is more picky about its dinner and prefers fruit over other types of rotting food. You may find yellow soldier fly larvae in your bin along with the offspring of black soldier flies.

Once your bin is seeded with black soldier fly eggs or larvae, it's a bit of a waiting game. You'll want to add small quantities of food scraps every day or two during this period since the grubs do best at digesting organic matter that has already started to break down. At first, these food scraps will act like a compost pile, wilting and decreasing in size slowly but surely. Then, at a certain point, the fly larvae get on the job and the voracious grubs eat the contents in mere days. At that point, your bin is fully operational and it's time to turn up the heat. (But do so in a figurative manner only—black soldier fly bins actually create quite a bit of their own heat and do best in shady locations.)

With a fully colonized bin, you should be able to see small, white grubs through the clear walls of your bin, so it's easy to keep an eye on what's going on inside. At this stage, you can add high-nitrogen food scraps or manure anywhere from daily through once a week, making sure you don't overload the bin. It should be easy to tell if you're giving your grubs the right amount of food since they'll keep growing without letting excess food build up within the bin.

After a couple of weeks of this type of treatment, you'll probably start to notice that the larvae have grown in size, with some turning black and migrating to the bottom of the bin. Now it's time to begin a weekly flushing campaign, pouring in enough water to fully swamp the entire contents of the bin before letting the liquid drain out into a leachate bucket. This leachate can be used like compost tea, providing a rich dose of nutrients for needy plants. But more importantly, the simulated rainstorm will prompt the largest larvae to crawl out of the bin and into the collection container, where you can easily gather the grubs to feed to your chickens or fish.

I have only a few additional words of caution before I turn you loose on building your own black soldier fly bins. Most importantly—prepare for some problematic odors. You obviously need to keep your bin outside since its ecosystem depends on constantly attracting female flies to lay their eggs ... and that's a good thing because even a well-managed bin will have some unsavory aromas. I was okay with the few weird smells wafting out of our porch-located bin, but I have to admit that I was less keen on the foul odor that rose from the leachate bucket if I didn't empty it regularly. And I definitely don't recommend using black soldier fly tea on potted plants living inside your house if you don't want to open all the windows and bear with some unpleasant aromas for a few hours.

Similarly, when the time came to apply black-soldier-fly compost to the garden the next spring, I was once again shocked by the aroma. I'm used to vermicompost, composted manure, and even composted humanure, all of which smell woodsy and pleasant. In contrast, the contents of my black soldier fly bin smelled exactly like uncomposted human fecal matter, which made me turn up my nose. While I assume there are fewer health hazards associated with black soldier fly compost than with uncomposted humanure, I'd still treat the former with caution based on scent alone. Perhaps you'd be better off adding black soldier fly compost to a trench in the garden like bokashi rather than top-dressing it like ordinary compost . . . just to be on the safe side.

Compost Tea

Compost tea provides plants with a quick dose of soluble nutrients.

I've now mentioned compost tea a couple of times, so I probably should give you a bit more information about this liquid fertilizer. At its simplest, compost tea is a liquid that contains the easily leachable nutrients from any sort of compost. So the leachate from a bokashi, vermicompost, or black soldier fly bin can be considered compost tea, or you can place a few cups of compost in a container with a gallon or so of water, mix the solids into the liquid, and then strain out the former to produce a homemade version of compost tea.

Of course, there are also more complicated versions of compost tea making the rounds. And to understand why you'd go to the lengths of following other types of recipes, you have to understand the various uses that you might have for this amendment in the first place. The simple version of compost tea mentioned above is highly effective for fertilizing plants in soils that have a low CEC and deal with high rainfall, meaning that the nutrients in solid amendments will quickly wash away without feeding your plants. In this scenario, you'll need to water your garden regularly with compost tea, a process often known as fertigation. And even if your soil's in good shape, you may choose to water in transplants with compost tea to get them off to a particularly good start.

Another purpose for compost tea in the garden is to provide missing micronutrients that don't move very well through plant tissues. In this case, you'll want to apply the compost tea (or seaweed extract) via foliar feeding, a fancy term that refers to spraying liquid on the plant's leaves. This type of application is most effective after you've pinpointed a specific micronutrient deficiency, possibly based on your plant's growth patterns but more likely from sending in a plant-tissue sample to a lab for analysis.

Up to this point, scientists and enthusiasts alike agree on the efficacy of compost-tea treatments, but the rest of this section will delve into the slightly murkier waters of aerated compost teas. In this scenario, your purpose isn't so much to provide nutrients to your plants as to breed large populations of beneficial microorganisms that will help your vegetables outcompete more harmful critters or otherwise reach their fullest potential.

To that end, you begin the same way you'd start making other compost teas, mixing high-quality compost (fresh worm castings are perhaps the best option in this scenario) with water in a five-gallon bucket. The differences begin when you feed the microbes, adding sources of simple sugars like unsulfured molasses, fruit juices, or cane syrup to promote bacteria and/or dosing the water with fungi-friendly complex sugars and proteins found in fish flesh, kelp, seaweed, soybean meal, oatmeal, or fruit pulp. Next, gardeners hook up an aquarium pump and stone to saturate the liquid with oxygen, after which they wait for a few days until the tea smells yeasty and good. (For more in-depth instructions on brewing your own aerated compost tea, check out *Earth Repair* by Leila Darwish.)

The finished, aerated compost tea is often sprayed on plant leaves in an effort to outcompete pathogens, but the liquid can also be used as a soil drench or poured onto a compost pile to seed the beneficial decomposer communities found there. The latter scenarios have the most biological potential, while foliar feeding seems dicey at best. After all, can microorganisms that spend their lives decomposing organic matter even survive in the sunny, dry environment of a plant leaf? And if they make it, what will they do without proto-humus to feed on?

As you can tell, I'm not so keen on aerated compost tea, so you won't be surprised to learn that I've never gone to the effort of brewing it for use in my own garden. However, I've found unaerated compost teas highly effective for feeding house plants, and exudates from worm and black soldier fly bins never go begging on our farm. Just remember—the quality of your compost tea depends on the quality of the initial compost. So use the best ingredients you have on hand if you want to provide nutrient-dense teas for your plants to gorge upon.

Chapter 16: Manure

Pros and Cons of Manure

Manure was the traditional source of soil fertility on the average farm a century ago. Luckily for modern organic growers, the simplicity of chemical fertilizers has turned manure into a waste product that is often free for the hauling.

I love manure. Composted along with an abundant supply of carbon (usually in the form of straw or wood-shaving bedding), the animal excrement turns into a rich source of both major and minor nutrients. In fact, in his book *The Gardener's Guide to Better Soil*, Gene Logsdon asserts that manure has a relatively unique ability to bind micronutrients into structures known as chelates, making existing minerals more available to plants than they might have been without the manure's assistance.

Meanwhile, you'll recall that applying manure to soil increases actinomycete levels, ensuring that nitrogen is more available to plants even when temperatures decline in the spring and fall. Of course, there's also the quality organic matter that jump-starts any garden's humification campaign, and my own experiences with remineralizing a pasture with animals suggests that manure application can neutralize problematic pH. No wonder studies have suggested that the fertilization effects of manure are much more long-lived than applying a similar concentration of nitrogen in chemical form.

But there *are* dangers related to applying animal manure in your garden. First, there's the potential for human health issues. Put simply, manure tends to carry the bacterium *E. coli*, which can make you sick. This danger is very low if manure is used properly since pathogenic bacteria die out quickly both during the composting process and when those organisms contact a microorganism-rich soil community. In most cases, simply composting manure before use and applying it to the soil just before planting will be sufficient to ensure your garden vegetables won't make you sick. But if your immune system is compromised, you can instead plan a few months in advance and spread manure on the garden during the autumn in order to fertilize spring lettuce and other crops that produce quickly and will be eaten raw.

The human-health danger of animal-manure use in the garden is extremely low, but soil and environmental repercussions should concern all of us. For example, poultry manure has to be used sparingly since this very hot (nitrogen-rich) manure acts similarly to chemical fertilizers in the garden. At its worst, poultry manure (and other manures if applied incorrectly) can release more nitrogen than crops need, promoting pests and weeds while also allowing nitrogen-based pollutants to run off into nearby bodies of water. Plus, these ultra-rich manures don't carry as much organic matter as manures from ruminants do, so chicken or turkey poop won't lead to the same long-term soil improvement benefits as the excrement from horses or cows.

Another downside specific to chicken manure is the potential for adding excessive amounts of phosphorus to your garden soil. The actual NPK value of animal-manure compost varies dramatically based on the species, the way the animal was raised, and the type of bedding used in the composting process. But, as one example, I purchased poultry-litter compost from an industrial facility a few years ago that was tested at an NPK of 3-4-4, meaning that the compost contained 3% nitrogen, 4% phosphoric acid, and 4% potash. What's most relevant to this discussion is the fact that the compost contains more phosphorus than nitrogen, even though plants need quite a bit more nitrogen than phosphorus in order to grow. In other words, if I applied this manure at a rate sufficient to meet my garden's nitrogen needs year after year, then I'd be overdosing on phosphorus.

Now, before you get too concerned about the phosphorus issue, if your mycorrhizal fungi aren't in good shape, then your plants are likely to need more phosphorus in the soil than you already have. Meanwhile, excess phosphorus is unlikely to cause a pollution issue since the nutrient doesn't leach out of the soil nearly as readily as nitrogen does. Instead, what might happen when you apply enough chicken manure to make your plant leaves green and well-fed is that you'll begin to refill your soil's phosphorus deficit. This is a good thing for a few years, but can become an issue eventually, so be sure to keep an eye on your soil tests if you use poultry manure as your primary garden amendment.

A final issue to consider when applying manure to your garden is the salt levels of the resulting compost. If you live in a rainy climate where rainfall naturally sucks sodium out of your soil, there's not much to worry about. But in the arid western United States, you'll need to keep an eye on sodium levels if you garden using large quantities of animal manures. The solution when these sodium levels begin to rise is to flush the nutrient out of your ground with a heavy round of irrigation . . . or just take a break from manure and use another type of compost for a while instead. With fifteen organic fertilization options to choose from in the preceding and succeeding chapters, you should be able to find something else to fill the gap.

How to Harvest Manure

Before we bought a pickup truck, we hauled manure in buckets in the back of our car.

Okay, the previous section may have made it sound like I'm down on manure, but that's entirely untrue. For the last decade, I've applied half an inch to an inch of composted horse manure to my garden beds before each planting, and my soil has thrived on that regimen. In fact, my husband and I keep adding more animals to our homestead in large part because we always need more manure.

But you don't have to own livestock in order to bring home this precious amendment. Just look for places where animals are cooped up—stables, dairy operations, even a neighbor with rabbits—and you'll find manure ripe for the picking. In most cases, the manure will be free if you load and haul it yourself, or the farmer might be willing to deliver a truckload for a small fee. And I should also mention that before we bought our pickup truck, we got away with hauling manure in buckets in the back of our car. So don't let lack of a truck bed hold you back from the manure hunt.

Characteristics of common manures

Manure source	Characteristics
Cattle	Cow manure is well-balanced, somewhat "cool," and low in weed seeds, meaning that you don't need to be as careful in your composting process as with some other manures. Dairy manure is likely to be richer in nutrients than beef manure since milk cows are fed richer foods. One cow produces, on average, about 11 tons of manure per year, enough to feed a one-acre garden.
Chickens	Poultry manure is hot (high in nitrogen) and can burn plants if not properly composted. But on the plus side, the manure tends to be low in weed seeds. Poultry manure is also especially high in phosphorus, so you should limit applications if your soil phosphorus levels are already elevated. Broiler manure is much stronger than layer manure while turkey manure is the weakest of the three. Among other poultry, duck manure is waterier and contains a lower concentration of nutrients per weight than chicken manure, but probably acts similarly once composted with bedding. Ten laying hens will produce about half of a ton of manure in a year, which is enough to fertilize about 2,000 square feet of garden.

Horses	Horse manure is hotter than cow manure, but not as hot as chicken manure. The amendment often contains weed seeds, making composting a must. One horse produces about 9 tons of manure per year, which is nearly enough to feed a one-acre garden.
Pigs	Since pigs are somewhat carnivorous, their manure has more potential to transmit diseases to humans. For optimal safety, use pig manure as you would humanure. A 200-pound hog produces about 3 tons of manure in a year, which is enough to fertilize a little less than a third of an acre (13,000 square feet).
Rabbits	If collected separately from the urine, rabbit pellets are cool enough to use without composting even though they're rich in nutrients. One female rabbit and her offspring will produce about a ton of manure per year, enough to fertilize about a tenth of an acre (4,000 square feet) of garden.
Sheep and Goats	Since sheep and goat pellets are relatively dry, they're easy to use in the garden. But the manure also tends to be relatively high in weed seeds and is somewhat hot from a gardening standpoint, so it's best to compost it before use. One goat or sheep will produce about a ton of compost in a year, which will fertilize about a tenth of an acre (4,000 square feet) of garden.

The table above gives you an idea of the characteristics of the most common types of manure you'll find on a homestead or nearby. Any of the manures listed (with the possible exception of pig manure) can be used in your garden, but be sure to follow my recommendations for composting the hot and/or weedy manures.

Actually, all manures are better soil amendments when composted, so even though rabbit-keepers will tell you that bunny pellets can be applied raw, you'll be better off ignoring their instructions. Perhaps most importantly, composting helps bind nitrogen into the organic matter so the essential nutrient is less likely to leach away—one study found that half of the nitrogen was lost from a pile of manure simply left out in the rain while very little was lost from a properly composted pile. If you're in charge of your own manure pile, you'll want to be sure to add sufficient bedding so you can't smell any ammonia (that's your soil nitrogen disappearing into thin air) and to keep the compost pile under cover if you live in a rainy climate.

That said, you *can* put raw manure straight into the ground if you do so far enough in advance to give the manure time to decompose. For example, if a neighbor offered me a truckload of raw manure in the fall, I'd definitely apply it to garden beds that wouldn't be planted into until late spring, and I'd also feel free to mix raw manure in with the wood in a hugelkultur system. Meanwhile, in the nonhypothetical world, I've been known to apply fresh goat-manure bedding to garden beds two to four weeks before planting a summer crop when I don't have composted manure on hand. Plants produced only about 75% as well as average . . . but isn't that better than no crop at all?

At the other extreme, if you don't have much manure and do have a big compost pile, you can use manure to get your compostables rotting at a faster clip. The highest-nitrogen manures are best for this, with chicken manure leading the way and human urine coming in not far behind. Alternatively, you can use manure to build a so-called hot bed to get early-spring seeds to grow despite frozen ground nearby. Just dig out the subsoil in a small area, lay down a thick layer of cow manure, then shovel the topsoil back in place for a natural heating pad that will help your lettuce sprout before anyone else's. Perhaps that's enough incentive to prompt you to track down manure . . . or to bring home a cow of your very own.

Deep Bedding

My goats like to help on manure-cleanout day.

Up to this point, I've assumed that you don't have livestock and are just in charge of handling the manure that another farmer has forked out of his barns and coops. However, if you're raising animals, then you can go the extra mile to make sure your livestock are happy and your manure is top-notch.

In most cases, the best solution for both animals and your garden is to use the deep-bedding method (also known as deep litter). This technique works best in a dirt-bottomed barn, where naturally occurring soil microorganisms can move in to turn the lower layers of your animal's floor into a compost pile. To begin, mound several inches of bedding material—autumn leaves, straw, or wood shavings—atop the bare ground, then continue to add more bedding daily or weekly as needed to keep the material that your animals are actually walking across clean and dry. As with piles of composting manure, your goal is to never smell ammonia, since that gas is not only a sign of wasted nitrogen but is also bad for your livestock's health. In addition, you'll need to be sure to add enough bedding to sop up the urine of everything except poultry since liquid waste contains half of the manure's nitrogen and most of the potassium.

Deep bedding has benefits beyond the eventual garden compost as well. The mixture of plant matter and animal manure will release heat as the lower levels decompose, which is a boon for overwintering animals in a cold climate. In addition, chickens can scratch through the bedding in search of worms and other critters that inevitably appear. Actually, some farmers find the technique so effective that they fill their cold-weather chicken runs with leaves a foot or more deep in the fall, essentially turning that area into a deep-bedding chamber that provides extra worm-hunting ground with no chance of winter mud.

Given this information, you might not be surprised to learn that, in most situations, the composting bedding/manure mixture is actually found to be healthier for livestock than cleaning out their living areas frequently. However, it's probably safer not to use deep bedding in kidding stalls since newborn calves and kids will do better if not dumped into microorganism stew as soon as they emerge from the womb. In addition, if you're not fastidious with your deep bedding, you could cause mastitis in milking animals with very dangly udders, so keep that bedding fresh.

In a perfect world, you'd clean out your deep bedding once a year and construct a compost pile using the mixture of plant matter and manure, allowing the materials to rot down into the perfect amendment to feed your garden. I have to admit, though, that I'm perennially low on manure and instead tend to use my deep bedding as-is in the fall or early winter as a high-nitrogen mulch that will soon decompose into compost in situ. Of course, uncomposted deep bedding has the same problematic characteristics as the various manures I outlined in the last section—poultry manure can burn plants and goat manure can be full of weed seeds. But if you know what you're getting into, deep bedding is a great way to turn the manure-management chore of the animal husbander into black gold for the garden.

Humanure and Urine

Both solid and liquid human wastes can be used on edibles . . . with care.

If livestock manure is such an excellent amendment for the organic garden, can we use human excrement in the same way? The answer is yes—and no.

The obvious problem with applying what's sometimes known as humanure to the garden is the very real potential to spread diseases. Chickens and goats share very few pathogens with humans, but every kindergartner knows you wash your hands after you wipe because you don't want your own excrement getting in your mouth. Since the plants you grow in your garden generally end up going straight down your gullet, there's an obvious disconnect here. Luckily, several solutions exist for this problem, ranging from the very simple to the very complex.

At the simplest end, many large-scale farmers currently purchase sewage sludge from municipal treatment facilities then apply that sludge to their fields. This purchased amendment has been treated to kill all pathogens and is considered safe ... even though heavy metals, pharmaceuticals, and other chemicals regularly end up in the processed waste. As an organic grower, I consider the choice of whether or not to use sewage sludge on my garden a simple "no" based on the presence of those chemicals.

On the other hand, collecting your own urine and pouring it on the compost pile is a simple "yes" for me. Unlike solid human waste, urine is nearly always biologically pure (the exception being if you're suffering from a kidney or urinary-tract infection). So as long as gardeners use pee while it's fresh, there are no disease issues to be concerned with.

That said, pee *will* burn your plants if not diluted (one part pee to ten parts water is the usual recommendation), and salts from frequent urine fertilization *can* build up in dry soils. If you water different parts of your garden with urine every time, though, you're unlikely to see a problem in a moderate to large growing space. Or, like I said, just pour the undiluted pee directly on the compost pile for a nitrogen boost that will speed up decomposition while ensuring that no pathogens wind up on your garden plants.

A funnel and milk jug were the first incarnation of my female urinal, but I soon changed over to a five-gallon bucket tucked in the corner between the porch and top step.

But how do you collect urine for use in the garden? Men can easily pee into an empty milk jug, while women will find it pretty simple to squat over a five-gallon bucket. In either case, the only important point is to use the urine in your garden before it begins to smell. As the name of one book on the topic—*Liquid Gold*—suggests, using pee in your garden is definitely low-hanging fruit for the organic gardener. As a result, I highly recommend this practice to anyone who has distant enough neighbors that they can set up a urine-collection system outside.

Moving on to the "maybe yes/maybe no" category of using human excrement in the garden, it's finally time to talk about my husband's least-favorite part of our nutrient cycle—home-composted fecal matter, also known as humanure. Some cultures apply humanure directly between row crops, but most consider that practice a bit dicey from a disease point of view. The safest choice is to use well-composted humanure around the base of ornamentals, while second safest (our practice) is a fall application of compost around the bases of fruit trees and berry bushes that won't bear until the following year.

In either case, notice that I wrote "well-composted." It's imperative that your humanure has achieved a temperature of 143.6 degrees for at least an hour, or 109.4 degrees for at least a month if you want to eliminate all risk of spreading human diseases into your garden through compost application. And I recommend spreading some mulch on top of the composted humanure while you're at it to make sure children or dogs don't play in the amendment. The mulch will also have the side benefit of speeding up humanure's colonization by beneficial fungi and bacteria, which do a great job of outcompeting pathogenic microorganisms.

Unfortunately, the specifics of gathering and processing humanure are beyond the scope of this book. If you're interested, I highly recommend Joseph Jenkins's *The Humanure Handbook* for in-depth information on humanure-composting systems, or you can check out our own composting toilet in my book *Trailersteading*.

I'll conclude by admitting that humanure has an ick factor that other sources of garden organic matter lack. But the amendment is safe and effective if used properly, and the process also keeps your excrement out of the waste stream. So, in the end, even my husband was forced to admit there's something to love about that.

Biodynamics

Biodynamic agriculture is based on the concept of holistic farm-ecosystem health.

While I'm on the topic of manure, I'd be remiss if I didn't at least mention biodynamics. Although my scientific background makes it very difficult to read some of the more wishy-washy descriptions of this farming practice, certain aspects of biodynamic manure processing might have permaculture potential once you strip away the mysticism. As an example, let's look at so-called biodynamic preparation 500, sometimes referred to more simply as horn manure.

Preparation 500 is the first concoction that most new biodynamic practitioners create since the amendment is recommended for improving problematic soil. Biodynamic gardeners begin in the fall or early winter by tracking down a cow's horn, along with enough manure from a currently lactating cow to fill said horn. The manurey horn is then buried, open end down, in soil that's been enriched with compost. The area is then mulched to prevent weed growth, and the preparation is allowed to rest for about four months.

By the time you dig up the horn, the manure inside should be well-composted and ready to apply to your soil. At this point, a non-biodynamic gardener would say she was creating a compost tea, although the biodynamic practice adds lots of biologically insignificant methodologies—stirring the manure into water in a particular pattern for an hour, then spraying the resulting liquid on the garden in the evening under a certain phase of the moon. Only a very small quantity of preparation 500 is required—about a handful per acre—and biodynamic practitioners will explain that this idea of a small volume leading to a large effect is based upon homeopathic principles.

It's tough to find scientific studies analyzing the efficacy of biodynamic preparations, but overall comparisons of biodynamic farms to traditional farms *do* tend to show dramatic soil improvements in the former compared to the latter. On the other hand, much or all of this difference may be due to the use of compost and manure since organic farms often stack up just as well as those managed using biodynamic principles.

In the specific case of preparation 500, I suspect that any biological effect results from beneficial microorganisms that colonize the manure as it composts within the cow horn. Perhaps the bone itself promotes certain species, similar to the way terra preta becomes more than the sum of its parts when animal bones, charcoal, human waste, and other forms of organic matter are combined in pits in the tropics.

That said, in the absence of further data, I've yet to give any biodynamic preparations a try on my own farm. After all, I'd rather spend my energy tracking down large quantities of horse manure than putting all of my eggs in the preparation-500 basket. But, just in case you feel differently, complete instructions can be found in several places online if you simply search for "preparation 500 biodynamics." And if you run a side-by-side, scientific experiment proving that preparation 500 does much more than seeding microorganisms in poor soil, I hope you'll get in touch and tell me all about it. I'm always glad to be proven wrong!

Chapter 17:
Tree Products

Why Wood?

Wood products are a great way to increase humus and beneficial-fungus levels in your soil.

Since lignin is one of the main precursors of humus, and since wood is one of the best sources of lignin, adding tree products to your garden soil is a no-brainer. And rotting wood doesn't just improve humus levels. The amendment also encourages fungi that will help your plant roots reach further into the earth, capturing phosphorus and other nutrients that are hard for plants to soak up on their own.

On the other hand, wood has such a high C:N ratio that fresh wood chips mixed directly into your dirt will tie up nitrogen as they decompose, leaving plants stunted. So be sure to follow the tips in this chapter to enjoy all of the benefits of wood as a soil amendment without running into nitrogen difficulties.

Wood Chips, Sawdust, and Shavings

If you know a woodworker, you may have found a high-quality source of wood shavings.

Let's start with acquisition of one of the most common tree products—shredded wood in the form of chips, sawdust, or shavings. Wood chips are easy to find if you live close to a well-traveled road and can flag down the local tree-trimming crews. These folks can save both time and money by dumping their haul into your yard, and after a year or two of slow decomposition, rotted wood chips make top-notch mulch around the bases of fruit trees and berry bushes.

Similarly, sawdust and wood shavings from lumber operations are a great boon to the garden as long as you're positive that none of the wood was treated with chemicals prior to being carved into shape. And these smaller chunks will decompose a bit faster than wood chips, allowing you to dust a thin mulch of rotted sawdust directly atop newly planted rows in the vegetable garden without worrying too much about microorganisms stealing nitrogen from your emerging seedlings.

As I mentioned above, though, a high C:N ratio is the main failing of wood products of any kind. As a result, you won't want to mix wood chips into your soil unless you add a significant source of nitrogen, which can be done by soaking the chips in urine or amending them liberally with composted manure. And I should warn you that even those quick fixes are likely to backfire if used in the ground beneath hungry vegetable plants.

On the other hand, trees and shrubs love the fungally-dominated environment created by a mulch of well-rotted wood chips spread directly on the soil surface. You'll know the wood chips are well-rotted when perhaps half of your pile has decomposed into small particles of rich, black humus. Mulch with this type of amendment, and your fruit trees will definitely thank you.

Rotting Logs

If wood chips aren't ripe for the plucking in your region, then punky (rotting) logs from several different sources will make a good addition to your soil. Those of you who cultivate mushrooms on logs will find that your harvests eventually peter out, at which point the remaining logs are perfect for use in the garden. Similarly, if some of your firewood crumbles instead of splitting, you'll know that the wood would be better turned into humus rather than heat.

Finally, if you live in the middle of a forest like we do, you might even commit a bit of time to hauling home punky logs that are rotting on the forest floor. In this scenario, just keep in mind that fallen logs are also an important source of fertility for the wild ecosystem. So use moderation when harvesting, and never transport logs over long distances if you want to prevent the spread of pests and diseases.

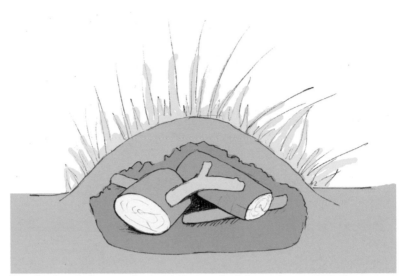

To make a hugelkultur mound, set aside the topsoil, pile logs and compost into the excavation, then shovel topsoil back on top.

So you have a pile of punky logs—now what? The most common way to utilize rotting wood in the garden is via hugelkultur, a method popularized by Sepp Holzer. Building a hugelkultur bed is simple. First, dig a hole in a new garden spot, pile in whatever wood you have on hand, then shovel the dirt back over top to create quality raised beds. Alternatively, if your water table is very high, you might instead start these hugelkultur beds on the soil surface, using topsoil from the aisles (or from elsewhere) to create taller beds that will keep your plants' feet dry while wicking up moisture out of the subsoil through the humus created by decomposing logs. At the other extreme, if you're gardening in sandy soil in an arid climate, you might dig out a bit of subsoil before piling in the logs then returning the topsoil, creating a sunken hugelkultur pit.

No matter how you build your hugelkultur beds, though, please keep in mind that the wood will likely use up nitrogen as it decomposes for the first year or two just as wood chips do when dug into the ground. If you're a patient gardener, you can plant cover crops (particularly legumes) onto the young beds during that period, further improving the soil so eventual edible crops will grow like gangbusters. On the other hand, if you're a normal, impatient gardener, be sure to plant more shallowly rooted vegetables for the first year or two and to top-dress more than usual with rich compost. It can also be handy to mix manure or compost in with the logs when creating the hugelkultur bed if you're in a hurry.

Either way, around three or four years after construction, hugelkultur beds really take off and become ready for prime time. At this point, you can treat them like any other garden bed and will find that even heavy feeders like tomatoes will be turbo-charged when treated to the results of buried, rotten wood.

Logs can be used to form garden-bed borders.

Over time, the log borders will begin to decompose, feeding the surrounding soil.

Another option is to use whole logs as edging around garden beds. The upside of this method is that if you use mushroom logs, you can see (and pick) the last few fruiting bodies that will inevitably pop up even after you've given up on a log as fruited out. Plus, the technique looks really pretty. And shallow plant roots thrive when they grow into the rotting wood that your garden borders decay to create.

My own experience consisted of using the log-border technique in a young blueberry patch, where I hauled rotting pine logs out of the woods as edging (and in an attempt to further acidify the soil). I was surprised by how quickly my bushes found their new nutrient source, as evidenced by the suckers that popped up along the logs' length within a few years. And the patch was definitely photogenic.

Unfortunately, I soon discovered that using logs as edging has a major downside—weed control. Even though I was careful to lay cardboard beneath my edging logs as a kill mulch before placing the wood, sturdy perennial weeds soon popped up on both sides of the logs. Without removing my edging, it was very difficult to root out the source of those weeds, so the pests kept returning year after year. Only when my husband began hitting the tenacious plants hard with the Weed Eater multiple times per growing season did the floral invaders along my edging logs finally come under control. So be forewarned—edging garden beds with logs will keep all the plants happy . . . even the weeds.

Stump Dirt

Stump dirt is the well-rotted heartwood found in the center of some middle-aged trees.

The next wood product I want to regale you with acts quite a bit differently from chips or logs. Stump dirt—the stuff found in rotten interiors of mature trees—is well enough composted that you can apply it directly to your garden beds for soil-conditioning purposes. However, it's hard to find very much stump dirt, so I instead save the amendment for use as potting soil during my seed-starting endeavors each spring.

If you want to follow my lead, you should first scan the hillsides for large trees that are starting to rot out at the base. Then, as you sink your hands into the compost within those decomposing trunks, you'll discover that not all stump dirt is created equal. Some is pale in color, a bit like slightly rotted sawdust, a sign that the amendment will steal nitrogen that your tender seedlings can't afford to give up. Instead, look for stump dirt so dark it resembles the very best compost or worm castings—that's the amendment you want to scoop up into a bucket and bring home.

Horned Passalus beetles seem to be at least partially responsible for high-quality stump dirt in our region.

Beetle castings are evident as distinct round balls that look like worm castings and are similarly high in nutrients.

So what makes stump dirt so special? When I first began rooting into rotting trees, I thought the miracle substance was created by fungi decomposing the heartwood in the center of old trees. And that probably *is* the case in some instances. But then I broke open an old stump in my garden and found a colony of Horned Passalus beetles (*Odontotaenius disjunctus*) hard at work munching on the old wood and pooping out perfectly round castings that looked awfully familiar. Which brings me to a second field mark you can look for when identifying prime stump dirt—if the humus holds together in little round balls, it's likely to be high in nutrients and perfect for potted plants.

Since the primary value of stump dirt lies in its fluffy, sponge-like nature that holds moisture and makes it easy for tender roots to push their way through, I recommend saving the amendment for plants that need it most. In my case, that usually means seed-starting or rooting grapes and other hardwood cuttings. In either case, I simply pull out any big chunks of wood that accidentally ended up in the organic matter, then I pour whatever remains straight into my plants' containers.

Once seedlings started in stump dirt have grown for a few weeks, they generally need more nutrients than the wood product can provide. At that point, I'll repot using a mixture of half stump dirt and half well-rotted horse manure, the combination of which will carry the plants through until they're ready to be set out into the garden. On the other hand, if I'm trying to keep a long-term potted plant happy (like a dwarf lemon tree that isn't hardy enough to spend the winters outside in the garden), I'll usually pot the plant up in pure stump dirt then feed it regularly using the compost-tea techniques mentioned in chapter 15. Remember—stump dirt is really about the texture, not the food, so be sure to provide other sources of nutrients as your potted plants grow.

Paper and Cardboard

This new garlic bed is a testament to the ability of paper and cardboard to expedite weed-free gardening. The bed was built atop sod the same day garlic cloves were planted, with two layers of processed wood preventing grasses from taking back over. As a first step, I broadforked the grassy aisles where I wanted the new bed to go, then I laid down a layer of corrugated cardboard to kill the plants underneath. I was redesigning the layout of this garden plot at the time, so I was able to shovel good topsoil from other beds on top of the cardboard for immediate planting. Then, as I buried each clove of garlic into the new ground, I laid a grid of newspapers around the planting spots so only the soil directly atop each clove was bare. Finally, I lightly scattered deep bedding from the goat barn onto the newspaper, topping the fertility layer off with a thicker mulch of fresh straw. The instant garden was ready to stand on its own two feet after being watered well (in this case by a week of solid rain).

While the more natural forms of wood are top-notch for soil conditioning, I turned to processed wood for mulching. Yes, I'm talking about paper and cardboard here, those waste products frequently found amid businesses and homes in an urban environment. And of the various forms of processed paper products that end up in my garden, corrugated cardboard is my all-time favorite.

When I sing the praises of cardboard so highly, I'm not kidding around. There's simply something special about corrugated cardboard in the garden that seems to transcend the box's simple structure. Perhaps the important feature is the lack of finish on the rough surface, the air spaces between layers, or even the glues that hold those cardboard sheets together. Whatever the reason, flattened boxes attract beneficial fungi like crazy and tend to break down at just the right rate beneath a straw or wood-chip mulch. In fact, when used as part of a fall-built kill mulch, cardboard shades out all weeds and then dissolves into the soil at the perfect time for spring planting.

Cardboard makes an excellent weed-retardant layer beneath homegrown mulches, like this buckwheat recently ripped out of the now-bare spots between young apple trees.

Flattened boxes are handy for new kill mulches, but they're an even better fit around woody perennials. Even with nothing on top except a rock or two to hold the boxes down, one layer of cardboard will prevent most weeds from poking up beneath your trees or berry bushes all season long.

Recently, I've expanded this method by kill mulching the soil just beyond the root zones of my perennials as well. If I lay down a cardboard kill mulch in autumn, I can lift off whatever remains the next spring to top up the mulch beneath my fruit trees. The newly bare ground prompts me to scatter buckwheat seeds, and a month later that cover crop is ready to be harvested and mounded up on the nearby trees' cardboard to build soil right where the trees need it most. Next, I plant another round (or two) of buckwheat to keep the bare ground weed free and growing its own organic matter in preparation for the day when tree roots eventually spread so far.

Moving on from my beloved cardboard, I've recently developed a soft spot in my heart for newspapers as well. As I mentioned in chapter 9, a two-layer thickness of non-glossy newsprint makes a great weed-prevention barrier around new seedlings in the spring. Add some straw on top and you may not have to mess with that vegetable patch again until harvest time. Equally handy is laying down newspaper atop a newly planted garlic bed, leaving six-inch squares uncovered for the emerging spears to pop up through. The paper layer prevents the profusion of chickweed and dead nettle that otherwise tends to take over even straw-mulched garlic beds, ensuring bigger bulbs in the spring.

Shredded junk mail and phone books make an acceptable mulch, but weeds tend to poke up through the paper if you don't include a kill layer underneath. The bright white of the mulch can be visually surprising for the first few weeks as well.

Shredded paper also makes a good bedding material inside chicken nest boxes.

Organic Soil Amendments

Junk mail has a place in my garden as well, although I doubt I'd hunt the amendment down solely for that purpose. White paper with black ink can be shredded and used to hold down kill mulches around perennials, or the fluffy paper product can act as bedding in worm bins or in chicken nest boxes. Meanwhile, thin cardboard boxes that house various food products can go through the same shredder to be used similarly. Just be aware that the thickness of both of these products makes them a bit too woody for use in the vegetable garden, and you definitely wouldn't want to mix either into the soil even around perennial plants.

The effects of mulching with glossy paper are striking. The broccoli plants in these pictures are the same age and variety, but the plant on the left was mulched with glossy paper while the plant on the right was mulched with grass clippings. Glossy paper stunted the former and made its leaves turn purple, a sign of plant stress.

Before I end this ode to paper and cardboard, I should discuss the reservations many organic gardeners have about using processed wood products in their gardens. First of all, there's the fact that glossy paper makes plants unhappy. The precise reason for this observation is unclear since in most cases, the gloss is due to a harmless (although potentially slightly radioactive) clay. On the other hand, binders and various other chemicals are also included in the production of most glossy papers, so it's not entirely surprising that plants tend to dwindle in their proximity. Or perhaps the problem is as simple as the gloss retarding water so the paper is less of a fully functioning part of the ecosystem. No matter the reason, I've learned my lesson the hard way—keep glossy paper out of the garden and your plants will thank you.

Colored inks and dyes are also sometimes eyed askance by the organic-gardening community. That said, in my own garden, I'm willing to include the occasional colored sheet or white page with colored ink since I know that the chemicals will be vastly diluted by my large garden. The potential issue in this case is heavy metals, which (unlike other pollutants) aren't broken down by beneficial fungi and can build up in your soil over time. So if you live in an area that already suffers from an overabundance of heavy metals due to nearby industries, previous rounds of pesticide or herbicide application, lead paint, treated lumber, or runoff from streets, you'll probably choose to completely eschew the use of colored inks in your garden. Better safe than sorry.

Colored and glossy paper aside, processed sheets of pulped wood have a very important place in the no-till garden. I suspect that once you try them out a few times, you'll turn into a voracious consumer just like me and will be unable to get enough cardboard and newspaper to feed your ever-growing appetite. Soon, your favorite birthday present may not be the gift inside, but the box your gift came wrapped within.

Caveat and Conclusions

A combination of log edging and rotted-wood-chip mulch created a vibrant soil for our young blueberries.

I'd be remiss if I ended this chapter without a few basic warnings about the hazards of using wood in the garden. As I mentioned earlier, rotting wood will initially immobilize nitrogen in your soil if not applied correctly, and you should also be wary of applying a few problematic types of wood to garden plots. Black walnuts are the most dangerous since they produce a compound that can prevent many other plants from growing nearby (although black raspberries, currants, gooseberries, elderberries, grapes, mulberries, persimmons, bamboo, and serviceberries are reputed to be immune), so black walnut wood is probably not a good fit for most gardens. Although not hazardous to other plants, red-cedar and black-locust wood is resistant to decomposition by microorganisms and may sit in your soil for a very long time in its original form rather than rotting as you'd intended. These species can make fine garden-bed edging, but would be a poor choice for a hugelkultur bed. Finally, you'll also want to skip treated lumber since that wood will not only resist decay, it can also release chemicals into the soil that you don't want entering your food chain.

With those caveats aside, all other types of rotting wood are good for plants and are especially good for garden soil. I can still tell the areas where I've applied rotten-wood-chip mulch even five or six seasons later because the dark topsoil is loose enough to use as a potting mixture. Meanwhile, when I recently dug up a six-year-old hugelkultur bed to improve drainage in the area, the difference between the zone where I'd applied wood and the surrounding soil was like night and day. Just keep in mind that adding wood to soil is a slower fix than many of the other techniques outlined in this book. Luckily, the eventual results are well worth the wait.

Chapter 18: Biochar

Terra Preta and Biochar

Biochar consists of charred organic matter seeded with nitrogen and microorganisms before being applied to the soil.

In a way, biochar should have been included in the last chapter since this amendment usually begins life as a tree. However, the topic is complex enough to merit a chapter of its own, especially since many gardeners believe that biochar is more than the sum of its parts.

The technique that has morphed into biochar began as a traditional method of improving soil in the Amazonian rain forest. As you may recall, organic matter in the tropics is hard to come by because warm temperatures and moist soil burn through detritus nearly as quickly as leaves hit the ground. So imagine the surprise of modern-day scientists when they stumbled across large deposits of dark soil (terra preta) in those same tropical areas. The patches of terra preta were several feet deep, were high in phosphorous, calcium, sulfur, and nitrogen, were rich in organic matter and microorganisms, and were also characterized by elevated moisture- and nutrient-retention capabilities.

As the scientists dug deeper (pun intended), they found that terra preta had been created by the human inhabitants of the rain forest, perhaps intentionally or perhaps simply as a way of disposing of waste products that would otherwise pollute their villages. Charcoal that began as wood, weeds, cooking waste, and crop debris was mixed with excrement, animal bones, and pottery shards in long trenches between 450 BC and 950 AD. The result was more impressive than the compost you'd expect. Instead, the rich soil of terra preta continues to grow good crops even hundreds of years after being created, and some folks believe that the quality soil regenerates naturally when native people excavate the black gold for use elsewhere.

As soon as news trickled north to the United States, gardeners began thinking, "I want some of that!" We slowly learned to create what has become known as biochar, often by burning wood in trenches directly in the garden earth. And since most of us won't be able to make true terra preta, the rest of this chapter covers the modern technique of biochar creation that can be used in all types of gardens, along with how we can tweak the common methods to more closely recreate the nearly magical substance found in Amazonian rain forests.

How Biochar Works

At its best, biochar is the ultimate form of stable humus. But the variety of changes that occur in soil treated with biochar are complex enough to merit a quick peek into the structure and chemistry of charred wood.

It's probably easiest for the average gardener to understand that the ash that inevitably comes along for the ride is the reason that biochar causes an immediate increase in pH within treated soil. After all, using wood ashes to boost the alkalinity of soil is common wisdom among organic farmers. But this effect is relatively fleeting and isn't responsible for most of the benefits that scientists discern after applying biochar to a farm field.

Similarly, we can easily visualize biochar's water-retention properties since a close-up look at charred wood makes each lump resemble a tiny sponge. As with most forms of humus, this ability to hold onto water during droughts is especially important for moisture and nutrient availability in sandy soils, and the characteristic certainly doesn't hurt even the best loams.

Still, water retention and a slight pH shift don't explain the vast changes in quality of terra-preta-amended soil. Instead, the complexities begin to build when you consider the chemistry involved. Like other forms of organic matter, biochar is negatively charged and naturally attracts important plant nutrients like calcium, nitrates, phosphorus, and silicates. In other words, adding biochar to your soil increases the soil's CEC, which is why biochar prevents nutrient leaching—the minerals are kept in the root zone rather than washing into the subsoil during heavy rains. This characteristic alone could be responsible for much of the improved soil quality in Amazonian terra preta, and the trait is especially important in the Pacific Northwest and in high rainfall areas of the eastern United States as well.

All of these factors help your plants grow, but probably the greatest benefit of biochar is its ability to increase populations of beneficial microorganisms in the soil. In fact, one study comparing terra preta to nearby, unaffected soil showed that the terra preta contained a completely different set of microorganisms than those found in the native ground. Other studies have shown that even run-of-the-mill biochar helps bacteria and fungi proliferate because the charred wood provides tiny nooks and crannies just big enough for these microorganisms to move into while being too small for predators to enter. In their protected dens, the beneficial microbes grow like crazy, especially if you make your biochar at a relatively low temperature so that the insides are coated with energy-rich tars for microorganisms to eat.

Meanwhile, scientists have also found that mycorrhizae (the fungi that attach to your plants' roots and help them rustle up hard-to-find nutrients) also gain a particular advantage when biochar is added to soil. Nitrogen-fixing bacteria love biochar too, but for a different reason—in this case, the effect is due to low-oxygen conditions where these anaerobic bacteria thrive. As a result, legumes create more nitrogen-fixing nodules when biochar is present in the soil and free-living, nitrogen-fixing bacteria also multiply, both of which mean more nutrients for your plants to eat without any work on your part.

But how many of these positive traits does the average gardener actually notice right away? After experimenting for a few years, I have to warn you that simply throwing charcoal into your dirt might not have much immediate effect, especially if your soil is already in relatively good health. In fact, if you have a limited amount of biochar available, I recommend applying it to your worst garden plot first since you'll likely see the most benefit in areas that are low in organic matter, excessively well-drained, or that suffer from a paucity of microorganisms.

Charcoal activated with urine showed little immediate results in my garden, although the dark color of the biochar boosted germination rates of early-planted onion seedlings.

And I should also warn you that, like uncharred wood, biochar has the potential to lock up soil nitrogen, so it's best to mix in a high-nitrogen amendment before throwing the charcoal in your dirt. At the same time, many gardeners also choose to seed the charcoal with microorganisms so the tiny critters can get a head start on colonizing their new living space space. This combination of adding nitrogen and microorganisms is often termed "activating" your biochar, a trick that can be accomplished by mixing the charcoal into compost heaps or by soaking it in urine.

The latter technique is fast and simple, but I have to admit that the only positive result I've seen from charcoal activated solely with urine is an increase in the germination rate and early growth of onion seedlings. This effect is almost certainly due to the warming action of the dark charcoal in the late-winter soil—nothing to sneeze at, but not the kind of biochar boom I was hoping to see in my garden. I'll write about other possible activation options in the next section if you want to get your biochar off to a faster start.

A spot where fireplace ashes were dumped several decades ago has turned into the richest soil in my garden.

Despite my own so-so results, other experiences suggest that biochar's effects on soil can build slowly but surely over time. A few of my garden beds are currently located in an area that was once the dumping grounds for ashes from the previous inhabitants' coal fires, as evidenced by the little chunks of charcoal (and lumps of unburned coal) that dot the soil. Although the texture of this area's soil is a bit grittier than the fluffy loam nearby, the earth is also darker and holds onto micronutrients much better.

How can I tell about the micronutrient-retention levels of the soil? A strawberry taste test, of course! Even though I top-dress our strawberry beds every year, I pull the plants out and begin in a new spot every three years because I can distinguish a subtle but noticeable decline in flavor when comparing year-one strawberries to the fruits of third year beds. On the other hand, strawberries that I planted in one of the biochar beds stuck around for about five years before I began to notice a decline in flavor. If you're like me and grow food because you know you can't buy anything that tasty and nutritious in the grocery store, this factor should be reason enough to add biochar to your garden soil. Just don't expect immediate results. Applying biochar is best for gardeners who are in it for the long haul and are willing to put in some effort now for better crops in the many years to come.

How to Make and Use Biochar

I mentioned previously that many gardeners produce biochar directly in trenches in the garden, and if you poke around the Internet you'll also find people building special biochar reactors that burn wood in the absence of oxygen (which is how charcoal is make). However, I have to admit that I look askance at methods that turn perfectly good firewood (or hugelkultur materials) into biochar. Instead, I follow the lead of the ancient Amazonians and make my biochar out of waste products that have already heated my home by burning to embers in my wood-burning stove.

How do you get biochar from a woodstove? It's simple. Like most people who heat with wood, I scoop out the old ashes every morning before I start the new flame, putting the leavings into a metal bucket for later disposal. Once a month or so, when the bucket is getting full, I wait until the morning's ashes have cooled completely, then I head outside to sift my biochar.

(As a side note, if you don't heat with wood, you might be able to collect ashes from a neighbor who does. He almost certainly has to dispose of his ashes and most non-gardeners consider the woodstove leavings to be a waste product.)

My husband built my biochar sifter by screwing hardware cloth onto the bottom of a box made out of one-by-six lumber.

To create your own biochar sifter, the only materials you'll need are a few pieces of lumber, some hardware cloth, and a handful of screws. My husband got fancy and made one end of my sifter into a spout to easily funnel charcoal into a bin, but you could get away with just creating a rectangle out of wood and attaching the hardware cloth to the bottom. The entire project should take no more than an hour or so and will cost you only a few bucks, even if you buy the wood new.

No matter what your sifter looks like, you'll want to process your stove leavings outside directly over your ash pile. Pour a few inches of ash into your sifter, hold your breath (or don a dust mask), and shake the sifter from side to side. The ash will fall through the holes while bits of charcoal (and some clumps of ash) will remain behind atop the hardware cloth. Pick out and discard the clumps of ash, then pour the charcoal into a bin for later use.

Your next decision will be to grind or not to grind? On the large scale, most farmers choose to powder their biochar since the process makes the amendment easier to incorporate into the soil using heavy machinery. But scientists have found that biochar particle sizes ranging from a twelfth of an inch to three quarters of an inch showed the same effects on crops, and fungi and freezing will both work to break down your charcoal chunks relatively rapidly once the amendment hits the ground. In addition, powdering your biochar can have unintended side effects, such as causing soil compaction and lack of aeration. So you're probably better off putting those chunks directly to work as-is, especially if your soil is on the heavy side (meaning that it's high in clay or silt).

Biochar comes out of our woodstove at the perfect size to apply to the garden.

As I mentioned previously, it's essential to activate your biochar before applying it to the soil. Pouring urine over charcoal is a quick way to counteract the nitrogen-sucking potential of fresh biochar, but the liquid activator will do little to promote microorganism growth. Those of you who produce your own worm castings will be much better off mixing biochar with vermicompost and letting the combination mellow for a few days since the rich, high-microorganism environment will get your biochar off to a better start.

When activating biochar with urine, fill a bucket with about four gallons of biochar then pour one gallon of urine over top. The biochar will snap, crackle, and pop like rice cereal as it soaks up the liquid. Afterwards, your activated biochar is ready for use once it soaks up the majority of the liquid.

Or if you have a compost pile and aren't in a big hurry, you can simply toss the charcoal in with your kitchen scraps—the chunks of charred wood will help aerate the pile while the compost fills crevices in the biochar with nitrogen and micro-organisms. If you live in a dry area, you might opt to soak the charcoal in water or urine before adding it to your compost pile to be sure the nooks and crannies are fully hydrated, but those of us who have to cover compost piles to prevent frequent rains from leaching away nutrients will likely be able to skip this step.

Alternatively, you can use the new method I'm trying out this year—tossing biochar down the hole in our composting toilet. While it's hard to tell which components of the original terra preta are responsible for the astonishing dark earth in the Amazonian rain forests, no one will argue that human excrement wasn't part of the formula. Of course, the downside of this technique is that you'll have to use more caution when applying the activated biochar to your garden. See the section on humanure in chapter 16 for more information.

Chicken bones make great biochar.

Another change I've made to our biochar campaign in recent years is to begin disposing of chicken bones in our woodstove, in essence creating chicken-bone biochar. First, I extract all of the good nutrition from the bones by boiling up a pot of broth for human consumption, then I wait until the woodstove fire is raging before throwing in the bones and closing up the damper. (In general, if you want to create more biochar, damp your stove down rather than running a hot fire. On the downside, a damped-down stove will burn less efficiently and will create more pollution.) I have high hopes that the calcium content of the chicken bones will make my soil amendments even more nutritious for the fruit trees who are slated to receive next year's humanure contribution.

When applying biochar directly to a no-till garden, I lay down the biochar on top of bare soil. In this photo, I'm applying biochar to only half of a bed in order to run a side-by-side comparison of soil that has and hasn't enjoyed the amendment.

Next, I add my usual dose of compost on top of the biochar.

I'll end this section with a few quick tips on how and when to apply biochar to the soil. If you activated your biochar by throwing it down the composting toilet hole or onto your compost heap, no more thought need go into the process. Your biochar will enter the soil along with the resulting compost as a matter of course.

On the other hand, if you opted to go the quick-and-dirty route of just soaking your biochar in urine, you can choose precisely where and how to apply the precious amendment. Since I don't till my garden, I generally prepare my seedbed by raking back the mulch and pulling any weeds, then I scatter activated biochar on top of the bare ground. After adding a layer of compost, I'm ready to plant.

In this situation, I recommend applying the biochar in early spring around crops that can use the extra heat boost from the soil-darkening effect. Similarly, the ashes that cling to biochar for its first few months will raise the pH of the soil slightly, so you might opt to apply your biochar in beds where you're planning to grow tomatoes, pumpkins, sweet corn, spinach, peas, cantaloupe, cabbage, or beets, all of which thrive in slightly alkaline soil.

Regardless of what you plant into your biochar bed, I've found that the long-term effects of top-dressed biochar take a few years to mature. The chunks of charcoal work their way down into the soil as worms and other critters move the compost around, and the earth slowly but surely grows darker and more vibrant with life with each month that passes.

Ashes

Our ashes are a waste product, primarily used as a goat jungle gym.

The astute reader will have noticed that I sifted out and discarded the ashes when making biochar, and I can see some of you wriggling in your seats as you cringe at my lack of thrift. "Why throw out ashes, when they're such an important soil amendment in their own right?" the hypothetical reader asks.

This seems like as good a time as any to mention when you might choose to apply wood ashes to your garden . . . and when the amendment will do more harm than good. Wood ashes act a lot like lime by making your soil less acidic, so you should never apply ashes to a garden unless you've had your soil tested and have found that your earth is too acidic. On the other hand, even if your soil-test results come back showing that you *do* need to lime the ground, I don't recommend spreading wood ashes just yet. Ashes also tend to be very high in potassium, which is a very important soil nutrient . . . but which can be present in excessive concentrations in certain soils. For example, my soil is naturally so high in potassium that remineralization texts suggest that I flush excess potassium out of my soil using gypsum. This is a clear sign that applying wood ashes would be shooting myself in the foot.

Okay, so your test results say that you're good to go in both the pH and potassium departments. How do you add ashes to the garden? Many people simply scatter ashes across the soil surface, preferably in the fall so the amendment will have plenty of time to react with the earth and to change its internal pH. You can apply ashes at other times of the year as well but will want to be sure to provide a few weeks between application and planting seeds since tender seedlings are quite sensitive to the abrupt chemical changes that ashes promote. Alternatively, you can add wood ashes to your compost pile, but do so in moderation for the same reasons you'd use care when adding ashes directly to your garden.

Your next question might be: How much is too much? Your test results should give you a figure for how much lime the lab recommends adding to your soil in order to adjust its pH, and that will give you a good starting point. While wood ashes can usually be applied at 1.5 to 2 times the recommended liming levels, many pros recommend sticking to the soil-test suggestions just in case. After all, wood ashes are more likely than lime to vary from batch to batch, and it's much easier to retest your soil and apply a bit more ash next year than it is to try to take that alkalinity back out.

As you might have guessed from reading this section, I'm less gung ho about ash application than I am about other methods of adding wood products to your garden soil. Sure, wood ashes can assist the health of your soil by increasing calcium levels and sweetening a sour pH. But the ashes should be used as part of a remineralization campaign rather than applied willy-nilly the way you might spread other sources of organic matter. So please see chapter 12 for more information before adding ashes to your own garden.

Chapter 19:
Leaves and More

Straw

Our most expensive gardening expenditure of the year comes when we purchase our annual load of straw.

Compost and manure provide instant fertility while wood products and biochar ensure long-term soil conditioning. But when the time comes for mulching the vegetable garden, I turn to leaves. Specifically, I prefer grass leaves in the form of straw.

There are only a few potential downsides of straw in the garden. The first is cost. Straw isn't cheap, although you can usually get a somewhat reduced rate by buying directly from a farmer when straw is in season. Here in southwest Virginia, many farmers grow rye for the express purpose of producing straw, with the harvest coming in June. Those of you who live in an oat- or wheat-growing region might find that your local harvest is a little earlier. We also get a second chance at cheap straw in early November when agritourism providers close up shop and sell their decorative straw to gardeners like me. Finally, gardeners can buy straw at the local feed store or big-box store, but these middlemen tack on at least a dollar or two per bale to cover their costs.

When your mulch sprouts weeds, you're in trouble. In this case, the problem was caused by straw harvested too late so the seed heads had already matured.

Once you track down a source of straw, you'll want to make sure you're really getting what you paid for. The first problem to consider is seeds. Plants grown to produce straw can be harvested in one of two manners—either the plants are allowed to mature all the way and the grain is threshed out to feed to animals or livestock, or the plant is killed at flowering time with no threshing involved. Either way, there should be few or no seeds in the finished product. However, if the threshing fails or if the producer thinks he's harvesting at bloom time but actually mows after seed has already set, then your straw may sprout grass that will make you every unhappy.

Luckily, it's pretty simple to prevent this troublesome issue. Just squeeze a few seed heads as you check over your bales, looking for flat and empty heads rather than those full of hard seeds. If you find seeds, return the straw to the seller or use it as bedding in the chicken coop—you definitely don't want rye popping up amid your vegetable plants.

What's the other potential downside of straw? Some producers are now using herbicides to kill the plants that will turn into straw, with the goal of producing an extremely bright yellow product. You might be able to tell the difference based on color alone, but it's safer to ask whether your straw was cut or sprayed. For obvious reasons, chemically killed straw isn't safe for use within your garden—yes, the herbicide *will* carry over and destroy your tomatoes.

Those caveats aside, I could use an almost unlimited number of straw bales in my vegetable garden since straw makes up the area's primary mulch. I lay straw down thick (a full flake in each spot) for late-fall and winter mulches since I want the weed-control layer to last until spring. In contrast, I'm a bit more sparing with summer mulches, although I still spring for enough straw to smother weeds. Finally, I use a very thin scattering of straw—light enough so you can still see the bare ground underneath in places—atop broadcast cover-crop seeds to confuse birds who would otherwise eat my oat and buckwheat seeds up.

Using that methodology, my garden thrives beneath the straw. Worms work close to the surface, moisture is always available for my plants, and a healthy crop of mycelium (the non-fruiting, threadlike form of fungi) is often visible on the bottom layer of each straw mulch. In the end, I figure the expense is worth the high-quality food and the much lower workload when weeding time rolls around.

Hay and Grass Clippings

Hay is best suited for use as animal feed.

Many new gardeners head out to buy straw and come back with hay . . . a mistake that they usually only make once. The difference between these two farm products is subtle but significant. Straw consists of the stems and leaves of a cultivated grain, and producers are usually very careful to make sure that the plant is either harvested before the seed matures or that the seed is entirely threshed out of the straw. The upshot is that straw is (or should be) seed-free.

Hay, on the other hand, is produced by cutting fields of tall grasses and weeds, many of which have already gone to seed. So if you spread hay across the top of your garden as mulch, you generally end up with a pretty good lawn. Not quite what you were looking for between your tomato plants.

As you can probably guess based on this comparison, hay is better suited to feeding your cows than to feeding your garden. But some lucky homesteaders report being able to buy so-called spoiled hay cheaply enough to make it worth jumping through the hoops to add the potentially problematic amendment to their gardens.

If you want to try out this method, you'll need to understand what you're getting into. First of all, I should explain that spoiled hay has generally been allowed to get wet (or wasn't dried properly in the first place) so molds set in and made the bales unsafe to feed to ruminants. One option is to use the spoiled hay as bedding in a chicken coop, where the birds will eat at least some of the weed seeds while the stems and leaves act to buffer the flock's high-nitrogen manure. Once composted, the manurey bedding should be at least moderately weed-free, causing no more problems than the slightly weedy horse manure we use on our own garden.

Another option is to put the spoiled hay beneath the cardboard layer of a kill mulch. As long as you don't churn up the ground in the future, the weed seeds will never end up close enough to the surface to sprout. And more organic matter deep in the earth is always appreciated by plant roots.

"But what about Ruth Stout?" the well-read gardener may ask. "She grew her no-work gardens in deep hay mulches. Why can't I?" Well, this is a regional difference in semantics. From all accounts, Stout's New England garden was actually mulched with salt hay, which consists of grasses cut from saline estuaries near the shore. While salt hay *does* contain grass seeds, the propagules depend upon the wet, salt-marsh environment in order to sprout and grow. So you can safely mulch with salt hay without seeing any of the weed problems that will arise if you mulch with more traditional hays made up of inland grasses.

If you're careful, you can grow mulch right in your garden using grassy aisles and a mulching mower. But be careful of weed seeds being sucked up into the bag.

Speaking of grasses, I'll end this section with one more related mulch—lawn clippings. I had a brief love affair with this amendment, but after being burned a time or two I'm unlikely to go back.

I'll start with the most dicey source first. Those of you who live in the city can sometimes find bags of grass clippings on the curb along with autumn leaves. Unfortunately, these finds are as tricky as they are enticing because the kind of lawn owner who bags and discards her clippings is usually the kind of lawn owner who applies herbicides and chemical fertilizers to her yard as a matter of course. So I'd treat bagged grass clippings as potentially hazardous but possibly good enough to go beneath the cardboard layer on a kill mulch or to be tossed into a chicken coop as bedding. In both of these cases, microorganisms will have time to break down chemicals before the composted grass clippings end up coming in contact with your plants' roots.

On the other hand, if you cut your own grass with a mulching mower, you can collect the clippings using a bagging attachment and know that they're entirely safe . . . from a chemical point of view. And in the spring, these clippings *do* produce a top-notch (albeit short-lived) mulch in the vegetable garden. High-nitrogen, spring grass clippings melt into your soil within a few short weeks, and the amendment feeds the surrounding crops in the process.

So what's the problem? Before long, your lawn plants will go to seed, and the mulching mower will suck up all of those seed heads right along with the grass leaves. Then if you're not paying attention and mulch with those seedy clippings, you'll end up with an even bigger weed problem in your garden than you'd have when mulching with hay.

After running into this issue a time or two, I let my husband take the mulching bag off the mower and return the clippings to the lawn. He was thrilled since the change made his machine easier to operate . . . and I bought goats to cycle those nutrients back into the garden in a more roundabout fashion.

Chop 'n Drop

Although harvesting takes some time, homegrown comfrey leaves produce an excellent fertilizer/mulch combo. This photo was taken one week after comfrey application.

Gardeners who want to expand their mulching campaign beyond straw and grass clippings sometimes turn to chop 'n drop. This catchy permaculture term refers to growing perennials specifically for biomass-production purposes within a forest garden, then cutting those plants at intervals to create an instant mulch around fruit trees and other edibles. The trick is selecting species that can be harvested multiple times over the course of a year and that won't compete too much with your edibles in the process. Unfortunately, I forgot to get my experimental species to sign that noncompete clause, so I ended up with a big bed of healthy comfrey and one ailing fruit tree in the middle that I later cut down. In other words, my intercropping experiment was a major failure.

More seriously, if you want to experiment in this direction, I recommend growing your mulch plants separately from your edibles. In this type of situation, comfrey turns out to be an excellent fertility producer if you can handle the prickly hairs and if you have time to cut and gather the clippings. As you can see in the photo on the previous page, comfrey leaves rot down quickly to feed happy vegetables. Just be sure you don't include even the tiniest portion of root or you'll end up with a comfrey patch in that location and will have to find somewhere else to grow your vegetables.

On a different note, leguminous cover crops can be used in a similar manner, and some of these plants have the benefit of being annuals that you can slip into a fallow spot in your main garden without making a long-term commitment to growing your own mulch. I particularly recommend soybeans and cowpeas in this scenario, although you should expect only one cutting annually for each crop. On the other hand, if you'd rather stick to perennials, alfalfa is reputed to be a good choice, although I found my small stand too difficult to harvest with hand tools. Perhaps next year I'll try red clover.

Grains are an even easier chop 'n drop choice, especially if you want to grow a serious weed suppressor instead of a source of fertility. I rake up the rye tops that my husband has cut with a Weed Eater in June to mulch around vegetables and our garden thrives beneath the homegrown straw. But before you get too excited, I have to caution that you need at least six times the cover-crop area to completely mulch a garden using this technique. Less-productive grains like oats and barley will cover an even smaller expanse.

As long as you harvest the plants before they bloom, ragweed makes an excellent found-mulch plant.

Actually, my favorite chop 'n drop plant to date hasn't been a cultivated species at all. Ragweed grows way over my head during our wet summers, and if I catch the plants just before they bloom, I can scythe down vast armloads then bring the biomass home to mulch along my berry rows. The ragweed does a pretty good job of weed suppression, but I'm usually happier if I lay down a thin kill layer of newspaper or cardboard before stacking my ragweed plants on top. During the years when I've applied ragweed mulches in midsummer, my berry harvests have been phenomenal.

Pollarding is a form of coppicing that was often practiced in common areas in Europe. Rather than cutting limbs to the ground, peasants harvested firewood from higher up in the tree. Pollarding ensured that branches could regrow out of reach of grazing livestock.

The final category of homegrown mulch comes from trees that can handle coppicing (being cut to the ground at intervals). One traditional application of coppiced wood in the garden is noted in *Good Farmers*, where Gene C. Wilken reports that Guatemalan farmers interplant elderberry bushes amid their vegetable crops as a matter of course. Every year, the farmers cut back the bushes to stumps, then use the harvested leaves and branches to mulch around crop plants. The leaves have a low carbon-to-nitrogen ratio (a lot like grass clippings), so they decompose rapidly, feeding crop plants while holding in water and shading out weeds.

Here in the United States, there are dozens of trees that show a similar ability to resprout after cutting, and I've tried a few of them as mulch within my own garden. The biggest problem I've run into during coppicing experiments is that the harvested branches are woody enough to prevent my mulch from matting down into a weed-repelling layer. So after the leaves melt into the soil to feed my crops, I'm left with a network of twigs that can be hard to weed around. Worse, when I got excited and mulched my plants with black-locust branches in an effort to top up my soil-nitrogen levels, I ended up poking myself with thorns every time I stuck my hands into that dirt thereafter. You're probably too smart to make such a newbie mistake, but I felt obliged to warn you anyway.

In the end, I decided that mulching with branches wasn't worth the hassle. Instead, I started spoiling our goats by bringing leafy branches to their paddock in the summer, ensuring that wild fertility would end up in our garden plot after all. Because when it comes right down to it, manurey straw really *is* the greatest garden amendment, so why not channel other sources of fertility through livestock in order to get there?

Tree Leaves

Tree leaves make a long-lasting mulch around perennials.

While leaves harvested green didn't quite make the cut for me, autumn leaves are in my never-can-get-enough-of category. I've used this prime amendment for various purposes in the past and have now settled on the chicken coop as the best location for their application. My reasoning is that straw is a good at soaking up goat "berries" and urine, but the high-nitrogen manure of poultry (especially of ducks and broilers) requires a more rot-resistant bedding for balance. In addition, leaves have the benefit of being small and scratchable, so chickens churn up the deep bedding for me, mixing their manure into deeper layers rather than letting the poop sit on the surface as it so often does with straw. Finally, autumn leaves often have little critters mixed in, which the flock particularly enjoys consuming during winter months when animal protein is harder to come by. All told, if I had my druthers, I'd use only autumn leaves in the chicken coop year-round.

If you don't have chickens (or have so many leaves you can branch out beyond this prime application method), there are several other options for leaf utilization on the homestead. As long as you don't live in a windy area, leaves can be applied directly onto the garden as mulch, especially if you shred them first to ensure the leaves mat down before the next breeze hits. That said, in my experience tree leaves are a bit too slow to decompose for use in the vegetable garden even though their C:N is technically the same as straw. Perhaps the issue is their waxy surface? Whatever the reason, tree leaves hit the fungal sweet spot, so they make a top-notch mulch around trees, brambles, and shrubs.

Autumn leaves also work as a great carbon balancer in the compost pile if your other primary amendment there consists of high-nitrogen food scraps. Alternatively, you can compost leaves on their own for a very humus-rich (but relatively low-nutrient) soil amendment if you have plenty leaves and don't mind the wait. Either way, you might want to steer clear of species with compound leaves, like ash and most types of nuts, since the thicker stalk that the leaflets attach onto is slow to decompose in most compost piles.

Finally, in years when my mother has gifted me with lots of bags of autumn leaves grabbed from the curb in her city location, I've stuffed the biomass between logs in new hugelkultur beds, used them to sop up waste in the composting toilet, and tossed a few in the worm bin for good measure. I should mention that these bagged leaves are usually a much safer bet than found grass clippings even if you don't know how the lawn-owner in question treated her yard. The worst I've come up with after years of accepting bagged leaves from all and sundry is a bit of trash in my leaves, plus one round of chrysanthemum seeds that did their best to take over the soil beneath an apple tree. A timely kill mulch solved the latter problem and it took me all of thirty seconds to pick out the trash.

I harvest bags of autumn leaves out of our woods each year for use in the chicken coop.

If you're more rural than urban, of course, you can also rake your own leaves out of the woods. When you do so, it's best to look for areas with little undergrowth to prevent weed seeds from coming along for the ride. And if you find big drifts of leaves in hollows, this will make your raking job that much easier. I like to gather a big pile of leaves then manually stuff them into a huge duffel bag that makes it a breeze to haul the leaves home. Since I love being out in the woods, the task doesn't even count as a chore.

When raking leaves out of the wild, though, there are a few factors you should consider. First, are you harming the forest? The answer is generally no, as long as you rotate your raking so you never harvest from the same area more often than once every three years. In fact, pine plantations in the south are sometimes managed to produce about 150 bales of needles per acre every two or three years without any apparent harm to the health of the trees, so you're actually following a well-traveled agricultural path.

Meanwhile, ecologists further north have studied the effects of turkey scratching (which acts very much like leaf raking) and have found that the episodes act to turn back the ecological clock for a short time in the scratched area. In general, some seeds of early successional species (like red maples) manage to sprout at higher levels in scratched areas, while some later successional seeds (like oaks) rely on leaf mulch and thus perish during the scratched year. But as long as you let tree leaves rot as usual in your raking spot next year, everything gets back to normal in short order.

Which brings me to the other question you might have—are some tree leaves better than others? You'll want to steer clear of black walnut leaves, of course, but most other species' leaves are top-notch as long as you match the right tree to the right application. Thin leaves like those falling from red maples and box-elders rot quickly, while leaves from black locusts and other legumes are particularly high in nitrogen, making both of these categories a good choice for applications around vegetables. Pine needles are a perfect fit for mulching blueberries because the needles tend to acidify the ground, and tougher leaves like those from oaks and beeches are more neutral slow-rotters that work well around brambles and fruit trees or in the chicken coop. Finally, sugar maple is my personal favorite leaf producer since its detritus is right in the middle rotting-wise and is also particularly high in calcium, meaning that the leaves hold up well in the chicken coop then turn into high-quality compost by spring.

The moral of this story is: if you ever want to get on my good side, bring me cardboard and tree leaves. Both make my garden soil sing, and they'll likely improve the quality of your homestead as well.

Everything Else

If you live close to the ocean, seaweed is an excellent soil amendment that's free for the gathering.

The tree-leaf equivalent for those of you who live close to the shore is seaweed. While it's frowned upon to harvest seaweed anchored to rocks, the dead material that washes up on the beach after storms is generally free for the taking. The gathered seaweed is rich in micronutrients and quick to decompose, making the material an excellent remineralization amendment, compost-pile contribution, or fast-rotting mulch.

The only potential downside of using seaweed in the garden is the salt that tends to cling to the plant material. One option is to limit your oceanic mulch to asparagus beds since this vegetable enjoys much more sodium than other plants can handle. Alternatively, if you're applying enough seaweed that you think the salts might be a problem, hose the organic matter down first (or let it sit out in a couple of rains) to ensure you don't shock your vegetables with too much sodium.

If you live inland and still want a water-based garden amendment, you might be able to track down mats of algae that grow in over-fertilized ponds. I've pulled these masses out of a small water garden to use as mulch and can attest to the fact that the amendment works very similarly to seaweed (although without the micronutrient boost since the algae grew in fresh rather than in salt water). You can also harvest accumulations of duckweed in the same manner in midsummer, although these tiny plants usually rot down so quickly they aren't generally worth scooping out of the pond.

Moving away from the water and into the home, food scraps are an obvious source of found fertility. You can compost your kitchen waste, of course, but the scraps are really too high-quality to use in that manner. Instead, feed them to chickens, who will turn the scraps into manure with a side of fresh eggs. Or use food scraps in a worm bin or black soldier fly bin to create other value-added homesteading products.

Coffee grounds are technically food scraps, but I separate these out since those of you who live in a city can often gather bucketsful from coffee shops. The grounds are very high in nitrogen, so they can be used to heat up a compost pile fast, or you can use the grounds to grow oyster mushrooms while also producing a high-quality compost. Worms and black-soldier-fly larvae are reputed to like coffee grounds as well.

If you'd rather purchase your amendments, many gardeners turn to peat, coconut coir, or humates. I tend to steer clear of this type of product because my garden is so big that I'd break the bank applying them in any meaningful manner, and because shipping and harvesting issues mean their use isn't particularly sustainable. However, all three have been shown to improve soil quality, so they might be worth considering if you need to get the most growth out of a very small space.

I could go on and on, but I'll stop there. Chances are there's an organic waste product free for the picking in your unique area. Whether that's peanut hulls, municipal compost, or pet hair, your job is to find just the right niche for each material on your own homestead. To that end, simply consider whether the amendment makes more sense as a source of fertility, as a soil conditioner, or as a mulch and you'll be on the right track for improving the soil and creating a happy, healthy garden.

Making Deposits in Your Soil Savings Account

The small changes you make today in your gardening practices can have long-term positive effects on your garden and on the world.

In the beginning, soil building may seem like a never-ending struggle. But the savvy gardener soon realizes that she's banking something far more precious than gold with every application of manure and straw. These amendments sock away organic matter that will allow her to contract her gardening area and effort in the future while growing just as much (or more) food. Her soil will be far less prone to erosion when the ground is mulched or is growing a healthy round of cover crops, and each molecule of carbon turning her dirt blacker will be one fewer molecule shifting our earth's climate in unpredictable directions. Finally, during those inevitable hard years when drought or lack of amendments hit, she can draw a bit of the interest from her soil savings account and still come out ahead.

I'm not writing theoretically here, either. After nearly a decade of improving what was once poor, eroded ground, my garden finally seemed to be on easy street in early 2014. I had my technique down pat and found it simple to grow all of the vegetables my husband and I eat in a year. In fact, the garden plot had become so rich that I was able to set aside large tracts for one of my favorite hobbies—cover-crop experimentation—and still had bushels of cucumbers and squash to give away to all and sundry.

Then troubles hit. My husband—the one who knows how to drive the pickup truck through our morass of a driveway without getting stuck and who has the strong back to shovel horse manure into said pickup—got sick and needed the summer off. Meanwhile, our straw supplier got his wires crossed and harvested a field of rye after the seeds had already set in the heads, meaning that the mulch I spread on my garden sprouted weeds rather than keeping troublesome invaders at bay. Then, once Mark was feeling better and I started to get the mulch situation under control, the weather decided to throw one more monkey wrench into the operation. It rained and rained and rained all fall and winter so we were completely unable to haul any new amendments back to our remote homestead.

I entered the spring 2015 garden year with extreme trepidation. Lack of mulch the previous autumn meant weeds were proliferating, and I barely had enough manure stockpiled to feed the first round of early spring crops, let alone our large main garden. Some of you would have wisely taken a year off, planting cover crops and sipping lemonade in a hammock all summer long. But my husband and I depend on our garden to feed us, so not planting wasn't an option. Instead, I applied what limited organic matter I had on hand, I planted seeds, then I begged the earth for forgiveness.

Soil high in organic matter will continue to produce good crops even if you have to lower your compost-application levels for a while.

And my vegetables grew. No, not quite as prolifically as in years past. But we always plant a bit more than we think we'll need to make up for inevitable rounds of pests and diseases, and that buffer was sufficient to fill our larder, bellies, and freezer while still allowing us to give away a moderate surplus to friends and family. Even without fertilization, my soil continued to produce.

How could that be? In preceding years, high-quality compost, manure, and mulch had elevated our organic-matter levels so dramatically that a 2012 soil test showed 5 to 9 percent organic matter in our vegetable garden. Three years later when trouble hit, humus levels were almost certainly even higher. And as you now know, organic matter acts like a reservoir of soil nutrients, with each percent releasing around 20 pounds of nitrogen per acre into your soil every year. Since most vegetables can get by on 100 to 150 pounds of nitrogen per acre, even my poorest garden plot had enough of this important nutrient to go around.

Of course, I don't recommend withdrawing from your soil savings account frequently, if ever. As soon as weather and husband permitted, I began returning organic matter to our garden at regular rates, and I also set aside large tracts for growing cover crops (particularly soybeans) to repay my overdraft fees. But the experience was heartening because it helped me realize that if a trouble year ever comes around again, our garden will continue to provide for us just as we've provided for it.

The moral of the story? In your garden, as in life, you get back whatever you pay in. So why not spend a little extra time now building soil with biochar, cover crops, or compost tea? Your crops, your family, and the earth will all appreciate your efforts.

Acknowledgments

As with my other books, *The Ultimate Guide to Soil* grew directly out of the homestead and associated blog (www.waldeneffect.org) that my husband and I share. In fact, you probably noticed photographs and observations from our blog readers peppering these pages. What may not have been so evident, though, was the ways in which these readers' thoughtful comments have also improved my thinking and impacted the contents of this book in more subtle ways. Dozens of people whose names don't appear on those pages deserve a huge thank you for sharing their own adventures, and this acknowledgment barely does their contribution justice.

Similarly, although I didn't give him credit, my husband, Mark Hamilton, took half of the photographs in this book, did most of the heavy lifting during my endless rounds of experimentation, and gave me time to write while he kept the farm from falling down around our ears. Plus, my long-suffering husband finally caved to my pleas and embraced the idea of milk goats, proving that he really is the perfect match for a homesteading wife.

Beyond the farm, my father, Errol Hess, provided a thoughtful read of the first draft of this book and suggested several important amendments to the text. Meanwhile, my mother, Adrianne Hess, and world's greatest friend, Kayla Scarberry-Jacobs, kept me supplied in cardboard, newspaper, and autumn leaves so I could experiment to my heart's content. Both of my parents also provided a photograph on demand—did you spot them? Finally, Meadow Creature supplied a free broadfork for me to try out (which had the unexpected benefit of allowing me to work off steam with in between bouts of editing). My garden and book are both better for the assistance of these kind souls.

Next up, the folks at Skyhorse did a perfect job crafting the product you now hold in your hands. From the big title that inspired me to write a big book to the beautiful cover and careful editing, I couldn't have done it without them.

Finally, I have to end this book by thanking *you* the reader. If you write a review on the retailer of your choice, tell a friend about this book, or simply make it all the way to the bitter end, I owe you a debt of gratitude. Thank you for reading—you are why I write.

Appendix:
Recommendations for
Further Reading

My Related Books

Although most of my titles revolve around homesteading, I particularly recommend *Homegrown Humus* as your next read since this text covers my trials and errors with cover cropping. In addition, *The Weekend Homesteader* gives tips on garden planning and worm composting, while *Trailersteading* includes a look at our farm's humanure-composting system.

General Soil Books

On the other hand, if this book merely whet your appetite and you want to learn more about in-depth soil topics, I highly recommend *Soil Science and Management* by Edward Plaster. This title *is* a textbook, so the price tag is high. But the book is chock full of pictures and is actually quite easy to read, so it will be a useful reference on your shelf for years to come.

Gardeners who are scared away by the academic bent of the former book might instead enjoy Gene Logsdon's *The Gardener's Guide to Better Soil* or Joseph Smillie and Grace Gershuny's *The Soul of Soil*. Meanwhile, Jeff Lowenfels and Wayne Lewis's *Teaming with Microbes* is a photo-rich biography of the microscopic critters you can't see with your naked eye but that make such a huge difference in the growability of your crops.

265

Moving on to more specific subjects, Ehrenfried E. Pfeiffer's *Weeds and What They Tell Us* is now back in print, with the subject matter being summed up perfectly by the title. Next, Robert Kourik's *Understanding Roots* is particularly handy for a scientific look at dynamic accumulators. Then, if my cover-crop book doesn't give you enough information on that topic, you might want to check out Sustainable Agriculture Research and Education's *Managing Cover Crops Profitably*, which can be downloaded for free on their website at www.sare.org/Learning-Center/Books/Managing-Cover-Crops-Profitably-3rd-Edition. Speaking of free resources, Steve Solomon's *Organic Gardener's Composting* is also available for free download at www.amazon.com/dp/B004TS8ZFG/.

Gardener How-To Guides

The next category of recommended books includes those that are a bit less scientific and are based instead on long-term gardeners' experiences and wisdom. In this category, I highly recommend Jean-Martin Fortier's *The Market Gardener*, John Seymour's *The Self-Sufficient Life and How to Live It*, *Sepp Holzer's Permaculture* by Sepp Holzer, and Steve Solomon's *Gardening When It Counts* and *The Intelligent Gardener*.

Other titles I've referenced in this category include *Weedless Gardening* by Lee Reich, *Gardening Without Work for the Aging, the Busy, and the Indolent* by Ruth Stout, *The Vegetable Gardener's Container Bible* by Edward C. Smith, *Aquaponic Gardening* by Sylvia Bernstein, and *Earth Repair* by Leila Darwish. Finally, Gene C. Wilken's *Good Farmers* is a scholarly but fascinating look at traditional farming practices in Mexico and Central America.

More about Organic Amendments

If you want to read more about some of the odd-ball organic amendments I mention in the fourth part of this book, you should turn to Adam Footer's *Bokashi Composting*, Binet Payne's *Worm Cafe*, Johannes Lehmann and Stephen Joseph's *Biochar for Environmental Management*, Joseph C. Jenkins's *The Humanure Handbook*, and Carol Steinfeld's *Liquid Gold*. In addition, I've included further resources in the website list that follows.

Soil Testing

NRCS Web Soil Survey: www.websoilsurvey.sc.egov.usda.gov/App/WebSoilSurvey.aspx

UMass Amherst Soil and Plant Tissue Testing Laboratory: www.soiltest.umass.edu/services

Logan Labs: www.loganlabs.com

USDA Extension Service Map: www.nifa.usda.gov/partners-and-extension-map

Hands-on Information

My blog: www.waldeneffect.org

The Color of Soil: www.nrcs.usda.gov/wps/portal/nrcs/detail/soils/edu/?cid=nrcs142p2_054286

Meadow Creature Broadforks: www.meadowcreature.com

Black Soldier Fly Blog: www.blacksoldierflyblog.com

Biopod Black Soldier Fly Composter: www.thebiopod.com

Make Your Own Free Bokashi Starter: www.bocashi.files. wordpress.com/2010/03/bokashicomposting1.pdf

Gardening With Biochar FAQ: www.biochar.pbworks.com/w/ page/9748043/FrontPage

Index